The Stomach Virus
and Other Forms of Family Bonding

The Stomach Virus and Other Forms of Family Bonding

Kathy Peel

WORD PUBLISHING
Dallas·London·Vancouver·Melbourne

Unless otherwise indicated, all Scripture references are from the New International Version of the Bible, copyright © 1978 by the New York International Bible Society; used by permission.

Other Scripture quotations are from the following sources:

King James Version of the Bible (KJV).

The Living Bible (TLB), copyright © 1971 by Tyndale House Publishers, Wheaton, Illinois. Used by permission.

New American Standard Bible (NASB) © 1960, 1962, 1963, 1968, 1971, 1972, 1973, 1975, 1977 by The Lockman Foundation. Used by permission.

Library of Congress Cataloging-in-Publication Data

Peel, Kathy, 1951–
  The stomach virus and other forms of family bonding / Kathy Peel.
      p.   cm.
    ISBN 0–08499–3477–X
    1. Motherhood.   2. Motherhood—humor.
  3. Family.   4. Family—
  Humor.   I. Title.
  HQ759.P43   1993
306.874'3—dc20   93-532
                                                                       CIP

3 4 5 6 9   LB   9 8 7 6 5 4 3 2 1

Printed in the United States of America

To John, Joel, and James—Incredible Guys.
I have the great honor of being their mother.

Contents

Acknowledgments

---

collaborate (kə lab⁄ ə rāt⁄), *v.* to work in conjunction
with another or others, to cooperate.

No author is a one-person show. I wouldn't have a
show without my collaborators. They make it happen. I
acknowledge them with great appreciation.

Bill Peel. When our house gets to the point where it
looks okay—only if you take your glasses off; when it's
been so long since I've fixed a hot meal that my family
feels noticeably healthier; and when I'm so exhausted, it's
virtually impossible to pry me from my desk chair—short
of telling me Kevin Costner's at the door, Bill faithfully
comes to my rescue and asks if he can help by picking up
clutter, fixing dinner, or enhancing a chapter. My answer
is always yes.

Dan Johnson. Any man who faithfully works for five
years with a compulsive, hyper-energized woman, and
believes enough in her dreams to give them focus and
flight, should receive a huge bonus. (Like I said, he believes in dreams.)

Kip Jordon and friends at Word Publishing. In my
mind, it's a classy publishing team who listens attentively
to some author's harebrained request to add her own personal marketing wing onto the building, but waits until
she leaves the room to fall laughing on the floor. The Word
team is a delight to work with.

Jan Johnson. Every author wishes for an editor who reads manuscripts faster than a speeding bullet, has more wordpower than a locomotive, and is able to leap tall expectations from the author and publisher in a single bound. My wish has been granted.

Introduction: What's a Mother to Do?

Women's roles have changed dramatically over the past thirty years. Before the mid-1960s, most young women went to college to find a husband. To them, a bachelor of arts degree was secondary to meeting the right bachelor. They dreamed of marrying Ward Cleaver, driving a wood-panel station wagon, and living happily ever after in suburbia.

By the end of the decade, a new breed of women moved into the dorm. I had the good luck or misfortune (depending on how you look at it) of being part of this changing generation. Bored with the thought of ironing boxer shorts and spending half their days studying meatloaf recipes, women of this era wanted *real* careers and equal partnership with their husbands.

By droves they enrolled in business, pre-med, and engineering classes—formerly foreign territory to women. The male students welcomed their new classmates with open arms—mainly because bralessness was in vogue.

I noticed that when older sorority sisters returned to campus for homecoming and witnessed this new spirit of freedom they acted appalled—but were secretly green with envy. When weekend festivities ended, the alumni corralled their screaming preschoolers into sensible family cars and drove back to neighborhoods of tract homes to resume predictable lifestyles.

Curiosity heightened among young suburban mothers as reports trickled back that women were graduating and actually landing jobs in sleek skyscrapers. News of feminine corporate success spread like wildfire at waterless-cookware parties. Many a housewife longed to trade in her station wagon for a subway pass. She dreamed of wearing sophisticated suits and high heels to important meetings. Her days would be spent writing memos, eating business lunches at fine restaurants, and answering only important phone calls.

While moving endless mounds of clothes from the washer to the dryer, she began planning her move to the marketplace—to do something *meaningful* with her life. "Surely there is more to life than measuring fabric softener and playing space patrol," she silently hoped. She didn't have a clue that the world of Wall Street might be a tad overrated. It was hard to tell that the savvy woman on the cover of *Business Monthly* had perspiration circles under the arms of her silk blouse, runs in her high-density support hose, and hemorrhoid cream around her eyes to shrink the bags.

Meanwhile, up on the twenty-seventh floor, a corporate woman's stress-filled world is growing more painful by the hour—and so do her corns. Night after night she works late—only to return home to a dark apartment to eat Noodle Helper alone. "I'd give up my corner office in a minute if I had any prospects of marrying, settling down, and having babies," she says. "What I'd give for the freedom to jump out of bed in the morning after a decent night's rest, give the house a quick once-over, and enjoy the day watching my children play happily together."

Trust me, this woman may be knowledgeable about market trends, but when it comes to understanding motherhood and what it takes to run a household, her mind can be summed up in two words: altered state. First, a word about babies: No doubt she thinks postpartum blues are a range of decorator paint colors, stretch marks are lines on the floor of her health club, and colic is a gourmet garlic substitute.

Little does she know a good night's rest is two hours of uninterrupted sleep. Giving the house a quick once-over means clearing a path with a snowplow wired to the front of the vacuum. And expecting to find children playing happily together is like thinking the press will discover Bill Clinton and Rush Limbaugh playing horseshoes after a picnic lunch.

So who's right—the woman who craves a career outside the home in the marketplace or the upwardly mobile professional who longs to spend her days on the home front? Since I'm smarter than I look, I won't pretend to be an outside expert on this issue. And as far as what motherhood means to you, I'm going to leave that up to you. I've learned over the years that arguing with women over an emotionally charged topic—whether to work outside the home, whether to choose private or public schools, etc.— gives me about as much joy as burning my neck with a curling iron.

However, there are some principles that apply to every mother—whether she's paid in sticky kisses or company stock, whether she's a happily married mom in an old-fashioned nuclear home or a single mom.

1. *Motherhood is serious business.* It is not only a great privilege to have children, but a big responsibility we need to take as seriously as career success.

2. *Every aspect of a woman's work is very significant.* Whether we're changing a diaper or closing a deal, our work has dignity, honor, and value before God.

3. *A woman's role in the family is powerful.* To a great extent, we create the atmosphere and set the pace in our homes. We also play an important part in the development of the lives under our care.

4. *The family is God's invention.* He knows best how to make it work, and he intimately cares about every aspect of each family member's life. He also gives us practical advice and relevant principles that directly apply to motherhood, child-rearing, family relationships, household management, and the personal development of each family member.

5. *We need God's help in balancing life's demands.* Whether we're office managers, family managers, or both, we are only human. We can't do everything by ourselves, but we can rely on God's help.

Since many of us do have careers outside the home, in reality, we balance two full-time jobs. We work hard and keep long hours. More days than not, we feel stretched to the limit trying to balance competing time demands from motherhood, family management, and career. Then, as if our daily stresses weren't enough, our lives become almost unbearable when unpredictable difficult circumstances arise. Even while writing this book, unforeseen situations have occurred that have made me want to throw up my hands and quit.

Actually I was feeling pretty cocky at the end of last summer. After setting my yearly goals (I operate on a school-year schedule), I mapped out each week of fall so that I could balance magazine article deadlines, speaking engagements, media interview schedules, and write one chapter of this book every two weeks—while keeping up with Bill and the boys' needs, running the household semi-efficiently, and fulfilling my personal goals. I looked good on paper. But my real life was another story.

It didn't occur to me that our house might flood and the floors would have to be refinished; or that my husband would hurt his back and suffer months of painful physical problems; or that a business deal would fall through— causing serious family financial problems; or that the transmissions in two cars would go out; or that the roof would spring a leak; or that the washing machine, the dishwasher, and the television picture tube would go out; or that the septic system would back up—just to mention a few things. There were plenty of days I threw myself across the bed and cried because it was so hard to write a funny book when life was anything but funny.

So what was this mother to do? I decided to turn to prayer—in a big way. And in doing so I found an entry in my prayer journal that I made some time ago.

> Each day, Father, I pray you would help me be the best mother I can be, and that you would give me the ability to lead a life of *courage*, that I would stand up for truth and be tenacious for righteousness, even when "everyone else's mom lets them . . ."; *consistency*, that I would live out the convictions I want my children to embrace and model a life of self-discipline— even when it would feel better to follow the easier path; and *commitment*, that no matter what happens— adversity, prosperity, calamity—I will remain committed to my husband and my children.

Courage, consistency, and commitment—you'll find these three Cs throughout this book. They inform every single point I hope to make—whether it's understanding the power of a mother, discovering and developing our children's designs, knowing when and how to discipline, teaching children how to get along, understanding how teenagers operate, passing on our values, or connecting in meaningful ways as a family.

This book is about being a mother and running a family—and what it takes to do the job well. Now lest you think I'm setting myself up as the model mother or state-of-the-art family manager, please understand I'm far from perfect. Don't look for pat answers on how to stop sibling rivalry, turn your child into a genius, prepare gourmet meals, and pour spiritual values into empty containers. Under oath, my kids will tell you that I've got a long way to go. Just today I took my seven-year-old in for his five-year-old checkup, my sophomore complained his jeans have been in the to-be-washed pile so long that he's outgrown them, and the mayor put our house on his "Clean Up the City" hit list. Xanadu it's not.

I may be short on pat answers and perfection. But I'm long on experience, learning, and empathy. This book is for you and for me—busy women short on time and energy, but long on problems. On the days when we feel like we're in over our heads, we need to remember it's an incredible privilege to have a family and to raise children. We need to be reminded of the critical importance of the role we play in nurturing our families and helping them connect in meaningful ways with each other, with the outside world, and perhaps most importantly, with their own talents, skills, and spirits so they become the persons God created them to be. And each of us can use some fresh ideas about how to create an atmosphere where our families can enjoy living, laughing, and learning together.

I hope as you read this book you will laugh at me and learn to laugh with and at yourself. Approximately three thousand years ago Solomon wrote in Proverbs 17:22, "A cheerful heart is good medicine." And Norman Cousins stated in *Anatomy of an Illness* that joyful laughter causes the brain to create endorphins that relieve stress and activate the immune system. Personally, I can use a dose of this kind of medicine on a regular basis.

At the end of each chapter you'll find a section called Family Matters. These are ideas and principles I've collected over the past twenty-two years of motherhood and family management. Some are a result of my victories; many I've learned through defeat. Use them to stimulate your own thinking and planning. But remember, fulfilling your role as a mother and family manager is a lifelong pilgrimage. Don't expect miraculous changes overnight. Just start by setting some simple goals and acting on a few ideas that seem like a comfortable fit for your family circumstances and operating style. Please don't try to implement them all at once. Your children might run away.

But above all, don't forget this: As in most issues in life—there's good news and bad news. In this case, the bad news is that we can count on more than our fair share of problems and pressures and will sometimes feel like we can't go on. But the good news is that God has promised to help us every step of the way. We only need to ask.

1

Motherhood 101

The night before our wedding, I lay in bed thinking about the changes in my life soon to take place. In less than twenty-four hours I would have a new name, a new address, and a new role. I would be a wife, a homemaker, and someday, I hoped, a mother. I was prepared—or so I thought.

After two full months of bridal showers and teas, I could have opened my own department store. Our prenuptial festivities made the inauguration look spur-of-the-moment. At linen showers I received sheets to fit any size bed, towels to wrap around any shape body, and enough blankets to warm the entire population of Iceland.

At lingerie parties I opened box after box of bra-and-panty sets, jewel-trimmed slippers to rival Zsa Zsa Gabor's, and multi-layer chiffon nighties in every color. (Note: In 1971 the pill was a relatively new approach to birth control. Many couples still practiced the see-if-you-can-find-her-under-the-layers method.)

But kitchen showers really pushed my domestic button. I was ready to set up house. If I wasn't given every kitchen gadget ever invented, Martha Stewart can't cook. And dishes . . . I had enough dishes to host a buffet dinner for the state of Tennessee. No matter if I had forty-two place settings, I kept them all. (Okay, I confess I returned one set of mugs given to me by a former boyfriend. I was afraid I'd see his eyes glaring at me in my morning coffee.)

Although I started married life with top-of-the-line paraphernalia, it never dawned on me that I didn't have the first hint about homemaking. Maybe it was when I dumped an entire cart of groceries on the parking lot beside my car. (No one told me I was supposed to wait for the next available sacker to take them out.) Or maybe it was the multicolor specks in a dip I whipped up. (The hand-painted cutting board should have included instructions to chop on the back side.) But I think it was when I used a rectal thermometer to see if my roast was done that Bill knew homemaking was probably not my strong suit.

Nine months after our marriage, Bill and I graduated from college. He enrolled in graduate school on the starve-as-you-go plan, and I decided it was time to broaden my horizons—as well our budget. Still on a steep household-management learning curve, I looked for a job where I could learn new skills, feel challenged, and do my work from our home. I became the manager for ninety-two apartment units.

"Don't rent to strange people," and "If you don't collect the rent money, you have to pay anyway" were my only instructions.

"No pro*blem*-o," I thought proudly as I shook the owner's hand. "You're dealing with a bona fide college graduate here." As it turned out, there were a lot of things I didn't learn in college.

My first day on the job I sized up a potential renter as she walked through the door. There was something about her that made me think her bust measurement probably exceeded her IQ by at least forty. When she turned to close the door, I noticed the skintight leopard jumpsuit gave her a noticeable wedgie. But she was nice enough—so I gave her the key to apartment 104. As she walked out, she told me she was an "endowment display expert." I didn't have a clue this meant she was a topless dancer. We didn't get much sleep the night the police came to take her away—which happened to be the night before her rent was due.

Then there were the newlyweds. They looked so young and innocent as they filled out the application together. It gave me a warm feeling to think I had a part in helping them settle into their first love nest together. I smiled knowingly when the wife took me aside and told me her husband worked odd hours. She asked that I not disturb them if the drapes were closed; they had to make the most of his time at home. "You know how new lovebirds are," she whispered and winked.

I'm here to tell you not a ray of sunlight ever peeped through their windows. I'd heard of raging hormones, but this was ridiculous. When it was time to collect the rent, I certainly didn't want to disturb them—or embarrass myself. I figured at some point they'd have to come out for groceries, so I waited and waited—until the day I had to turn in the money. Only then did I realize they had lived scot-free for one month and moved out overnight.

At the rate people were leaving without paying rent, I couldn't afford much more of this kind of a challenge. And I'm not sure how many new skills I'd learned. But it sure made me want to try my hand at something else. Teaching school had to be easier than this.

Although I wanted to teach, schools that would consider me as a teacher were limited since I did not have a teaching certificate. I was almost ready to give up when I found a private high school that not only wanted to hire me, but asked me to start the next morning. It crossed my mind that I should ask why their average teacher tenure was three weeks, but I didn't. I needed the job.

You will understand me when, as a woman who believes all people are created in the image of God, I tell you these kids were a test of my theology. Take fifteen-year-old Jerry for example. He came to school every day smelling like a distillery. He was the kind of guy who thought Beethoven's Fifth was a bottle.

Another student was Rob, which was not short for Robert, but signified his favorite hobby. This boy was born with a silver spoon in his mouth—with someone else's initials on it. Rob attended school when he wasn't in jail.

But I'll never forget Chuck. I'm not sure if Chuck was his real name, but since he brought nun-chucks to school every day, it seemed appropriate enough. Chuck started the semester wearing a 24-karat gold ring through his nose, but he lost it in a poker game the third week of school. He gave new meaning to paying through the nose.

The school was dirty, and the parking lot was crawling with drug dealers. During my teaching career, I never used the restroom at school, never walked to my car alone, and never left food or drink lying around for fear it would be laced with LSD. Yes, it was a tough situation. But I learned some invaluable lessons there about kids and family life. Not one of these kids came from a home where love was expressed. They seemed shocked to know that someone—especially an authority figure—cared about them and their world. And when I praised them for making even the smallest bit of progress, I could tell by their response that hearing encouraging words was a foreign experience. It was exciting to watch as they began to make positive changes toward a new image of themselves. I made a mental note to remember this when we had our own kids.

One would think teaching troubled teenagers would stifle my motherly instinct. Instead it became stronger.

"Bill, could we try to have a baby?" I asked one night.

"Oh, I guess we could give it a whirl," he said, holding back a grin as he headed for the bedroom.

"Not *now*," I snapped, "I want to talk this through."

"Okay, Honey, what's on your mind?" he asked.

"Well, I was never around many babies growing up, and I don't know the first thing about managing a family. Do you think I'd catch on to motherhood?" I asked sincerely.

"Kathy, don't worry. We're both well-educated adults. We'll just read all the latest parenting books, study the principles, and formulate our strategy. And I'll do everything I can to help you—starting now," he smiled and led me down the hall.

It's doubtful a woman can know beyond a shadow of a doubt when she's ready to become a mother. But there are some telltale signs. You know your biological clock is ticking when:

—Your husband takes you on a date to a nice restaurant and you start cutting up his meat.

—You get the nesting instinct and thoroughly clean your house—losing your chance for Stephen King to film *Murder by Mildew* in your bathroom.

—You strike up conversations with women who are pregnant (and unfortunately a few who aren't) and ask them how much longer until their due date.

—Your milk comes in when you see a commercial for Puppy Chow.

—You're thirty years old and tired of wearing a training bra. (Pregnancy does have its advantages.)

When my obstetrician called to confirm my delicate condition, I made the decision to take excellent care of myself during my pregnancy. I wanted to be healthy and to look like my exercise instructor—who began getting a little thick through the middle in her eighth month. (I have since decided women like this should be locked up.)

I voraciously read books about caring for my body and the child inside me. Some authors said if I ate wisely and exercised moderately, I would not gain more than twenty pounds. They lied. By the seventh month I had thighs in two zip codes.

But not to worry. I read that lovemaking burns 125 calories, and I felt sure that after the baby came our relationship would change from *Romancing the Stone* to *In the Heat of the Night.*

I also read that a mother could burn up eleven hundred calories a day by nursing her baby. That was excuse enough for me. I bought a nursing bra.

I would like to pause here and share my feelings about nursing bras. They're as ugly as sin. You'd think the designers would understand that after eight weeks of abstinence, many women want to feel sexy again. The one time in our lives we're well-stacked—and all we have to show it off is a homely contraption. I considered sewing some fur on my nursing bra—kind of a Frederick's of Hollywood look—but I thought it might make the baby sneeze. Then I thought of making my own nursing bra out of leopard skin, but I didn't want to give our newborn an identity crisis. I figured nursing mothers who really wanted to look sexy could go for a braless wet t-shirt look—*au naturel.*

I didn't, of course, know about nursing bras while I was pregnant. I learned that later, along with a *few* other things—like how nursing pads make nice coasters for drinks. When I wasn't eating everything in sight that didn't move or reading books about raising perfect children, I went through my last trimester in a state of blissful anxiety. The blissful part was thinking about becoming a mother; we were going to be a "real" family.

The anxiety part was wondering if my baby would be all right. Would it be born with the usual number of fingers and toes, with all the parts in working order? And would I be able to love him? her? it? the way I knew a child should be loved? I didn't want to bring any Chucks, Robs, or Jerrys into the world. I wanted to raise the perfect, loved and lovable child.

When my due date approached, I packed my suitcase, put some finishing touches on the nursery, and to Bill's amazement, cleaned out every closet and drawer in the house. I was prepared—for everything except giving birth via Cesarean section—which turned out to be about my seventy-fourth favorite experience. It ranks somewhere between receiving a registered letter from the IRS and being hit broadside by a moving van. Women who have their babies the regular way nauseate me—especially when they trade episiotomy stories. They're worse than fishermen. I say you don't know pain until you've been the victim of a student nurse learning to install a catheter. After her fifth try and my fifth scream, I realized this young woman didn't understand the meaning of a place for everything and everything in its place.

But it doesn't matter if a woman has endured the physical pain of childbirth or the incredible personal and emotional pain of not knowing when or if she can adopt a baby, it's a universal truth for all mothers. The first time we hold a newborn infant in our arms and witness the miracle of new life, we forget about all the pain and tribulation. It's one of those rare moments in life when we realize something divine has taken place—and it's bigger than our finite minds can comprehend. As we begin to love and nurture this tiny life, we feel in partnership with God, the Creator of life.

David wrote in Psalm 127:3, "Children are a gift of the Lord" (NASB). This verse was especially significant to me at the births of our three children. For some reason God allowed each of our three boys to flirt dangerously with death when they were born. Nineteen years ago I checked into the hospital thinking I would have a normal delivery. For six hours my room was more like a party than a labor room. Unknown to the medical staff, John's umbilical cord was wrapped around his neck. As a nurse monitored his heartbeat during labor, she noticed it became dangerously slow. She knew something was wrong. In a matter of minutes I found myself in the operating room undergoing an emergency C-section—singing hymns out loud to bolster my faith. The doctor miraculously got John out in time to avoid brain damage.

Having motherhood almost snatched away from me before it began made me realize all the more the tremendous gift I had been given. As I took John home, I knew I was on a divinely commissioned mission.

The next gift came four years later. I knew things were not going well when I felt my OB make the incision. The anesthesiologist had not given me enough anesthesia. I was in such pain and shock, I could not even cry out. Finally the medicine took hold. When the doctor got the baby out, I heard the nurse say, "Mrs. Peel you have a baby *boy*." Kathryn Elizabeth had a penis.

By the rate of the heartbeat the doctor and the labor-and-delivery staff had predicted our baby would be a girl, so we didn't even have a boy's name picked out. When I left the recovery room, the nurse let Bill and me have a peek at him. We decided he looked like a Joel Andrew— and we jokingly said we'd keep him.

That evening, however, our joking stopped. The pediatrician came to my hospital room to tell me there was a fifty-fifty chance Joel would not make it through the night.

Joel was a beautiful baby. He entered the world at a strapping nine pounds, four ounces. But he had one problem: He could barely breathe. The doctor called it respiratory distress syndrome—which meant Joel's lungs did not manufacture the necessary lubricant needed at birth to breathe properly. His little chest caved in with every labored breath. It was agonizing to watch him strain so hard to breathe. I cried a lot, and I prayed a lot. My heart broke when I heard the nurses carting other babies to their mothers at feeding time. I knew mine was barely hanging on to life in the intensive care unit. Finally, on the third day we got the wonderful news that Joel's lungs had started to function properly. We took him home on the fifth day, and once again I knew I held an incredible gift in my arms— God's child, given to me to nurture and love.

Over time, I forgot my feelings of fear and trauma. Seven years later we decided to ask for another gift. I became pregnant. At thirty-six weeks, I checked into the hospital as my doctor tried to discourage early contractions. But James thought he was ready to get on with life. He was born three weeks before his due date. In the delivery room, Bill and I relived past traumas as the doctor turned to us and said, "He's not ready." James too had severe breathing complications.

That cold March day an ambulance took James to a large hospital in Dallas with a special intensive care unit equipped to handle infants with serious problems. Bill was with him every moment—touching, talking, and singing to James, and praying to God for a miracle. He called me regularly to update me on James's progress—which was usually none.

I was able to travel on the sixth day, so Bill came back to Tyler and drove me to Dallas—not knowing if we'd be able to bring James home. In this special hospital unit we saw infants who were extremely sick, small, and deformed. We met many hurting parents. Some knew their babies could not live long—but they stayed beside the tiny bed, gently stroking their baby's skin, softly singing, and lovingly calling their tiny one by name. Our baby was one of the few who took a turn for the better.

When I saw James for the first time, he had tubes, needles, and monitors everywhere. I longed to hold him to my breast, but couldn't because a tube ran down his nose. The eighth day God answered our prayers and his lungs started working on their own. We watched as they unplugged the monitors and pulled out the tubes. James had his first good cry. Incredibly, the next day we brought James home—acutely aware we had undeservingly been given another precious gift.

I don't know if it's a mother's instinct or the traumatic experiences that instilled in me an intense desire to be the best mother I can be to these precious gifts of life I've been given. My guess is every mother feels this to some degree.

I doubt there's a woman anywhere who begins her role wanting to be a mediocre mother and raise an average child. Most mothers secretly hope their child will grow up to be president of the United States—or at least a major corporation.

Actually, first-time mothers are easy to spot. Their conversations go something like this:

"Well . . . ," one mother flips her hair and lowers her voice, "I don't want to brag, but little Susie ate strained squash at five weeks, so we *know* her IQ will be over 150."

"How nice," the other responds with her nose in the air. "Actually, my husband and I have made an important decision. Not a drop of anything foreign will touch our child's lips . . . I plan to nurse for three years." (Note: Plastic surgeons love this kind of woman.)

You just don't hear comments from new moms about how they're failing at their job or how slow their babies are progressing. On the contrary, the conversations overheard between most mothers of newborns revolve around their astute mothering skills and how *their* baby is faster, bigger, smarter, quicker, happier, sharper, keener, and brighter than any other child who has ever lived.

Actually it's a great asset for a child to have a mother who desires the best for him or her, who believes big things, and dreams grand dreams. But why, over the years, do the dreams die? When does motherhood get unbearably hard? What happens between the delivery room and the dorm room that causes relationships to crumble? How can children smothered with love as infants grow up disliking who they are? Why do they lack ambition? Where did they learn to disrespect authority and compromise their beliefs?

We certainly didn't plan for it to happen this way, and we begin to wonder why it did. Was it too much television? The kids down the street? Working too hard at our jobs? Fighting with our mates in front of the kids? Divorce? Where we lived? Where they went to school? Where we did or didn't go to church? Or were we just not good enough mothers?

By nature we want to say "If only . . ." and look for a person or situation to blame. But there are no easy answers, and there are precious few rational explanations about why kids turn out the way they do. However, explanations and blame don't change things. When we struggle to explain what went wrong or blame it on anybody or anything, including ourselves, we're making things more difficult, not less. The best we can do is to do the best we can, work at leaving our past sorrows and hurts in the past, and wake to each new day being the best moms we can.

Since I'm not a sociologist or a child psychologist by any stretch of the imagination, I can't quote exact statistics about which circumstances impact a child's life the most profoundly. And I don't know specifically which negative influences affect personality development to the greatest extent. But I do know a mother's attitudes and actions and the atmosphere in the home have a profound influence on her children.

Like most moms, I want to enhance my children's intellectual, physical, and social development, provide opportunities for them to learn to be creative and resourceful, and help them grow up with a healthy self-image. I want to see them doing things they enjoy with confidence, so they learn that there's more to life's work than making money. I want to teach them the importance of self-discipline, instill in them a strong value system, and prepare them to make smart choices.

I want them to be able to love themselves and others. I want them to feel a sense of responsibility to be the best they can be and to share their skills, resources, and love with family, friends, and strangers. I want to love them in a way they can understand, and I want to plan regular times for our family to have fun together. I want our kids to enjoy our home and hang around here with their friends. I want them to be able to laugh at themselves and life.

And, I also want to cry.

Many days I feel completely stretched to the limit by the responsibilities of motherhood. When I feel like this, I've considered trying to escape. I've toyed with the idea of keeping my own tank of nitrous oxide handy. After all—why should getting a root canal be the only peaceful time in my life?

Most of the time, though, I come to my senses and remember there are three more intelligent things I can do to help me in my role as a mother.

First, I stay on a sharp learning curve about motherhood. Over the years I've read countless biographies of successful people—looking for information about the homes they came from and the mothers who raised them. I've devoured many good parenting books—trying to gain insights from the experts. And I've written pages of principles in my journal from studying the lives of parents and children in the Bible; there's a lot to be learned from their failures as well as their victories. I've also picked the brains of older mothers I admire—asking them to share their wisdom about motherhood.

Second, every day I ask God to help me with my job. Why I would even entertain the thought that I can be a good mother without God's help is beyond me—but in the past I did. As our family grew and the judgment calls got tougher to make and things got more complicated, I found myself putting Jeremiah 33:3 to practice on a regular basis. "Call to me and I will answer you and tell you great and unsearchable things you do not know."

Third, I have faith I will be the best mother I can be. This may sound simplistic, but it's true. Over and over, historians, psychologists, and theologians tell us we become how we see ourselves in our minds. Solomon, the wisest man to ever live, wrote in Proverbs 33:7: "As he thinketh in his heart, so is he" (KJV). What this means to me as a mom is this: If I have the attitude, "I don't know a thing about preschoolers, but I'm going to learn everything I can and be the best mom I can be—because this is an important job," then I'll probably be a pretty good mother. But on the other hand, if I harbor fear and think, "I'm afraid I'll be a failure as a mother of teenagers," chances are I will. An interesting story underscored this philosophy in my mind.

After fifty-seven years on the high wire, Karl Wallenda fell to his death at age seventy-three. In an interview, his wife discussed his last and fatal walk. She said that for three straight months prior to this walk, all Wallenda thought about was falling. This was the first time he had even entertained the thought of falling, she said. He put all his energies into fear of falling, rather than into walking the tightrope. What he feared came to pass.

There are a lot of fearful aspects about motherhood. It's a huge responsibility and a highly important position—for which no one is fully qualified. But to worry anxiously about motherhood—to my knowledge—never helps, and it only makes a child nervous to experience an anxious mother. Instead, we should relax and take our cues from the One who wrote the job description in the first place. Then we have nothing to fear. Motherhood becomes an incredible privilege and one of the greatest blessings of life, a gift from the Creator.

Family Matters

I don't know where you are in your role as mother. Maybe you'd just like to be one someday. Perhaps you're right in the thick of it—wondering if you'll ever have another peaceful moment in your life. Or maybe your kids are grown and you have wisdom you can share with those of us who are still in the process and could use some help. Wherever you are, I would like to suggest that you think about the following Family Matters—what they mean to you and what they could mean to your children. Maybe one or two will spark a fresh perspective in your own life, or you could use an idea to encourage another mother.

Take time to sit down and write each of your children a letter. Include your hopes and dreams for them and tell them how much you love them. Save the letters for graduation or wedding presents to your children. You can do this whether your children are infants or older.

"What the mother sings to the cradle goes all the way down to the coffin"—Henry Ward Beecher. Begin the habit of singing hymns to your young children while you rock them to sleep. The truths of the words will become indelibly etched on their minds.

Start a collection of good books about raising children. As you read, make notes of principles you want to remember and keep them in a journal. Bookstore clerks, librarians, and your friends are all good sources for book ideas.

"The hand that rocks the cradle is the hand that rules the world"—William Ross Wallace. Remind yourself regularly that to have a major role in the development of a human being is an incredible responsibility. No matter what your career is, motherhood is a very important job. It should not to be taken lightly.

§ֻ.

Evaluate your home and your family's activities to discover what and who, besides you, is influencing your children as they grow up. Studies show one of the most critical aspects of human development is the effect of repeated viewing and listening. Look for quality movies, books, and music your family can enjoy together.

§ֻ.

"The great thing in this world is not so much where we are, but in what direction we are moving"—Oliver Wendell Holmes. In what direction are you moving? Talk with your children and your spouse about your hopes and desires for your family.

§ֻ.

Seek out a wise, older mother to be your mentor. "A single conversation across the table with a wise man is worth a month's study of books"—Chinese proverb.

§ֻ.

We are given the privilege of influencing our children through thousands of small daily acts. Through these acts we help build their characters. What small act of love can you perform right now?

§ֻ.

Whether you are a new mother or an old hand at mothering, understand that part of your role means being flexible when unexpected events occur. Consider writing this sentence on a card and keeping it handy to remind you to stay cool in unpredictable times: The only predictable thing about children is that they are unpredictable.

ఌ

"The best academy, a mother's knee"—James Russell Lowell. As a mother, you can be your child's most influential teacher. Make a plan to teach your children something or to learn something new together.

ఌ

Read *The Blessing* by Gary Smalley and John Trent (Pocket Books,1990). This book is filled with practical ideas about how you can be a blessing to your child.

ఌ

Invest in a good camera and take a lot of pictures of your children. Display them throughout the house and at your workplace. This is a good way to let them know you are proud to be their mother.

ఌ

"An ounce of mother is worth a ton of priest"—Spanish proverb. What does this proverb mean in your life?

ఌ

"Behold, children are a gift of the LORD; / The fruit of the womb is a reward" (Ps. 127:3 NASB). Take time before you go to bed each night to thank God for each of your children.

ఌ

If you're a new mother trying to get used to your new schedule and lifestyle, turn potentially frustrating hours into productive think time. My friend Peggy Zadina spent many long hours in the middle of the night rocking her colicky infant daughter. It was then she developed the idea for *The Organizer*, a time-management notebook specifically for women.

§a.

"My mother was the making of me. She was so true and so sure of me I felt I had something to live for—someone I must not disappoint. The memory of my mother will always be a blessing to me"—Thomas A. Edison. Do something today to let your children know you are sure of them.

§a.

Don't get down on yourself when you make mistakes. No one ever has been or ever will be a perfect mother. What's important is that we keep trying. Remind yourself of this daily.

§a.

"For God hath not given us the spirit of fear; but of power, and of love, and of a sound mind" (2 Tim. 1:7 kjv). Don't fear your role as a mother. It is a divinely commissioned position you don't have to fulfill alone.

§a.

"The precursor of the mirror is the mother's face"— D. W. Winnicott. Smile when you speak to your children—even when they are tiny. It will help build a positive self-image.

§a.

Begin a prayer journal for your child. Pray for him or her regularly about every area of life. I pray for my boys' intellectual, physical, spiritual, social, and emotional well-being using Luke 2:52 as a model: "And Jesus grew in wisdom and stature, and in favor with God and men."

❧

"God has not called me to be successful; he has called me to be faithful"—Mother Teresa. Strive to be the best mother you can be, but remember that you cannot control how your children turn out.

❧

If you were an only child, if you're uncomfortable with children and unsure of your role as a mother, or if you're a stepmother trying to love and nurture the children you've been given, be honest about your feelings before God. He cares and wants to help.

❧

"In our terror of becoming destructive mothers and fathers, we refuse to be parents at all. We abdicate parenthood and turn over our responsibilities to strangers."—Madeleine L'Engle. No one can do a better job of raising your children than you. When you are fearful, turn to God.

❧

"I don't think much of a man who is not wiser today than he was yesterday"—Abraham Lincoln. Never stop learning about motherhood. Every stage has its own set of challenges.

❧

"The future is something which everyone reaches at the rate of sixty minutes an hour, whatever he does, whoever he is"—C. S. Lewis. Every day with our children is important in determining their future. Do something today to make their future bright.

2

No Two Children Are Alike—Plus More Reasons to Be Thankful

*W*hen my children get their own attorney (and it's only a matter of time), they will have an array of grievances for which they can take me to court.

James, being the third-born, will no doubt sue for age-related discrimination or unlawfully withholding information. Tired of running up and down soccer fields every Saturday morning with his older brothers, I told James soccer was banned in our city the year he was born. He contends every mother is legally bound to provide her child with equal opportunities given to other siblings, the child's order of birth or the age of the mother at birth notwithstanding.

Joel has a fair personal-injury case—since I let him roll off the bed on his head at age four months. But I think he'll have a better chance with a property-damage suit. He has an extensive evidence exhibit of all his clothes I've ruined in the wash over the years.

But John will definitely walk away with the most cash because he's the firstborn child.

Why firstborn children don't form a union is a mystery to me. With all the unfair rules, overzealous discipline, and show-Aunt-Barbara-how-intelligent-you-are performances forced upon them by first-time mothers, I think they could ask for some serious maternal-malpractice damages.

Actually, it's a miracle firstborn children grow up with any degree of emotional stability. They're the guinea pigs that must endure our trial-and-error methods of learning to mother.

One of the first crises every new mother encounters as her child grows from infant to preschooler is potty training. For me, this experience turned out to be about as joyous as dropping an iron on my foot. Every day of the process brought new challenges and tests of my endurance quotient.

I read that little girls mature earlier and are easier to potty train than little boys. Out to prove the experts wrong, I became a goal-driven woman. I was dead set on potty training John by his second birthday. Wrong-o.

There are three important points every mother needs to know as she begins to potty train her child. First, she needs to decide what terms she will use in the teaching process. Actually, after reading everything ever written on this topic and interviewing several experienced mothers, I learned there's a wide variety of opinions.

Some approach potty training very seriously. To them, mothers who use terms such as "pee and poop," "go big potty," or "number one and number two," are foolish and irresponsible. Maybe I'm out of touch, but there's something about hearing a two-year-old say she needs to defecate that doesn't sit quite right (no pun intended). As for my own upbringing, I'm sure my mother's using the term "go shu-shu" has nothing to do with my need for a straitjacket.

With my children, I decided to go the initials route: "TT" and "BM." I don't think there's anything psychologically harmful about using these terms—unless your preschooler cannot pronounce consonants clearly. In our case, "TT" worked fine, but "BM" came out—so to speak—"Mia" (pronounced mee-a). This can be very confusing to a babysitter or if your child is a guest at someone's house and walks around in circles repeating "Mia, Mia, Mia." They wonder if this is his grandmother's nickname or if he's been watching Italian movies. This term caused unnecessary trauma once on a family vacation when we stopped for the night at a motel called the Casa Mia. The kids cried because they thought we were spending the night in a big bathroom.

The second thing every mother needs to decide is what type of reward system she will use when the desired behavior occurs. I talked to mothers who kept candy jars in the bathroom and others who went so far as to offer a trip to the toy store for cooperation. But the prize for the strangest method goes to the mother who put her child's pet bird in the bathroom to give him some company while he sat. This gave new meaning to the term "stool pigeon."

I tried playing mood music, letting the faucet trickle, and promising to let John wear special Incredible Hulk underwear for a successful bathroom visit. I even bought a Tinkle Star potty chair that was supposed to play "Twinkle, Twinkle Little Star" upon victory. We never heard the song. After months of frustration on my part, I gave up and he potty trained himself.

It was then that I recorded in my journal the third and most important thing every mother needs to remember about potty training: Don't worry about it. Come to think of it, potty training is no longer an issue in the lives of most adults I know.

Trying to do everything by the book and wanting to give our firstborn children every advantage, we smother them with the opportunities, experiences, and activities we deem most important. High on the priority list of every new mother is giving her preschool child early socialization opportunities through a play group with children of similar ages.

The thing to remember about play groups for first-born children is that it doesn't take long to size up and label the other mothers. They're as stereotypical as the characters out of a midday soap opera. No matter if you move across the country and join another group. The faces and names will change, but the personalities will be the same.

The organizer of all play groups is Linda Left-brain. She's the type who administrates her child's entire life in ten-minute segments. Every morning she follows the same routine. The first hour of her daily appointment book looks something like this:

7:00	Wake up Melinda
7:10	Juice
7:20	Oatmeal and vitamins
7:30	Bath
7:40	Dress
7:50	Free play
8:00	BM

At the first meeting of the play group she hands out bylaws, safety rules, disciplinary standards, health authorization forms, personal information on each member, five hundred creative projects to do with kids, and her menu plans for the next five months—in case the other mothers have a busy day and need a quick idea.

The next mother you'll meet is Susan Sickly. She's the only mother I know with a standing appointment with the pediatrician. One cough—Stevie has pneumonia. An insect bite—it's a rare skin disorder. A missed bowel movement—he has a blockage. He falls down while playing swing the statue—inner-ear balance problems.

When she drops her squeaky-clean child off at your house, she'll run her finger across your coffee table, then rattle off thirty-seven types of dust Stevie is allergic to. She has an extensive vocabulary of medical nomenclature and carries a pharmaceutical dispensary in her shoulder bag. During play group she waits in her car with a pair of binoculars and a portable oxygen tent.

Sally Social began grooming little Allison for her "coming out" before she actually came out. The week she was born, Sally signed her up for the "right" preschool, tap and ballet, piano lessons, junior tennis at the club, "White Gloves" classes, and started a list of sorority sisters she could count on to write recommendations.

Allison's designer-look wardrobe is enough to make any other child feel like an orphan. But it's her birthday parties that take the cake—as they say. You show me a child who attended a birthday party hosted by Sally Social, and I'll show you a child who thinks her own mother is a cheapskate. Pin the tail on the donkey, musical chairs, and bubble-gum party favors lose their pizzazz once you've experienced a party with a Ferris wheel set up in the honoree's backyard, a seventy-five-dollar-an-hour clown who brings his trained chimpanzee, and individual Barbie-doll favors.

The last mother in the group is Carrie Cum Laude. She's the kind of mother who had the alphabet tattooed across her chest so her baby could learn while he nursed. Her life ambition is to make sure Holmes Barrington Hillford V—Quint for short—is the brightest child born in this century. She started multiplication flashcards at six weeks, reads bedtime stories from the encyclopedia, and plays "French Made Easy" cassettes during his afternoon nap.

At play group, the other children create choo-choos and bang-bangs from Legos. Quint builds a perfect scale replica of Monticello. When the kids dress up in capes and argue over who gets to be which super hero, Quint opts to be Ross Perot. At lunch, the other children scream for peanut-butter sandwiches, chips, and lemonade. Quint orders grilled boneless chicken breast, steamed baby vegetables, and sparkling water.

But despite the mothers' idiosyncrasies and insecurities, the children usually rise above them and have a positive play-group experience. It's too bad firstborn children have to take their mothers through more stages.

Another hoop new mothers want their children to jump through is athletics. In their minds, signing up the child for the sport of the season is not optional—that is, if the child is going to amount to anything.

In our part of the country, T-ball is one of the first team sports young children play. Take a random poll of kindergartners to find out why they thought their mothers signed them up for T-ball, and 4 percent would say their moms are interested in the development of their hand-eye coordination. Twenty-seven percent would say their mothers want some free time in the afternoons while the kids go to practice. And 69 percent would say their mothers are sure their child is the next Lou Gehrig.

We never realize at the onset how much it costs for a young child to have an organized sport experience. First there's the initial sign-up fee, then the uniform, cleats, baseball glove, child-size bat, batting glove, team pictures, twenty dollars' worth of chocolate bars your child is supposed to sell but instead leaves in the trunk of the car to melt, not to mention your time spent running back and forth from practices. You also need to add in a one-night stand in the refreshment booth selling nachos made from faux cheese and stale chips. All in all, you can count on spending about 137 bucks and seventy-eight hours of your time—so your child can make clover chains in center field.

If I told you mothers of firstborn children are more serious about winning the games than the kids are, I would be telling a half-truth. They are hell-bent on winning. I've seen mothers climb chain-link fences to cuss out umpires who call their child out. They feel just because their kid ran from second base back to first, he should be given another chance. I've seen mothers sobbing because their child struck out. And I know mothers who don't speak to each other when their children are on opposing teams.

By the time James, our third-born, started playing T-ball, Bill and I had changed from overzealous to somewhere between sluggish and lazy. Our philosophy became, "Why run when you can walk, why walk when you can stand, why stand when you can lean, why lean when you can sit, and why sit when you can lie down?" Maybe our age was starting to show.

The first summer James played T-ball, he played on a team filled with firstborns. Just watching the parents was enough to give me heavy eyelids. While Bill and I sat in our lawn chairs, they stood behind the dugout and read inspirational passages from Nolan Ryan's biography. In between games they drove their kids to batting cages to practice and watched how-to baseball videos. They also videotaped every minute of every game. Over the summer, these kids starred in more film footage than John Wayne.

By the end of the season, the parents were emotionally and physically exhausted and the children didn't know or care how many games their team won. But they had a patient and positive coach who made them feel good about themselves, plus they had a good time. And that's what mattered.

Over the years I must have read more than a hundred articles on stress and stress management. Whole books are devoted to discovering the stress in your life and relieving it. Every last one of these articles and books lists stress factors—death, divorce, financial crisis, overwork, unemployment, illness, moving. As far as I know, none of them lists one of the biggies for mothers of young children—Halloween.

Halloween is about my 267th favorite celebration. It ranks somewhere between Bunsen Burner Day (March 31) and Tiny Tim's birthday (April 12). My family can always tell when Halloween is approaching. I turn into Cat Woman.

I don't know why I take my hatred of this holiday out on my family, but I do. I cry if I see a jack-o-lantern. I pitch a fit when I have to buy twenty pounds of hard candy. And I hate, hate, hate getting the stupid costumes together.

Why my children always want to be characters like King Ptolemy of the Nile for Halloween, I'll never know. Maybe they do it to torture me. They start planning their costumes eleven months in advance. By September, if the parts are not coming together, they threaten to stop breathing. Of course, most of the costume pieces require a professional tailor and headpieces or masks that are only available from the wardrobe department of Warner Brothers. To casually ask if this year they might consider a cheap plastic costume from the discount store is like asking if this is the year they might like to come down with hepatitis. A good Halloween for me is when I only have to spend $125 (and that's a conservative figure) for period costumes from *Les Misérables*.

If my children realized the leverage they had in negotiations because of Halloween, they could lead the life of Riley. You show me a child who's willing to forget Halloween, and I'll show you a child with an open credit line at FAO Schwartz and a lifetime exemption from chores.

I'm telling you, Halloween puts a lot of peer pressure on a mother who thinks hem tape is something the choir director uses to mend sheet music. And as luck would have it, in every preschool PTA I've ever belonged to, all the other mothers have taken private sewing lessons from Adolfo.

It's embarrassing to admit how much I gave in to peer pressure in a lot of areas when my kids were young. Where was Nancy Reagan when I needed her? Someone needed to remind me to "Just Say No." To be honest, I was one of the leaders of the pack of insecure mothers who wouldn't accept anything less than the best for their children. "Best" was usually trying to force my children to be something they weren't created to be.

Although most mothers won't admit it, they understand the universal pecking order. Kids with brains, beauty, brawn, and bucks usually make it to the top. It takes a mother with a strong sense of self-worth to recognize and communicate to her children they are special, even if they don't have excessive amounts of these attributes. It's all too easy to take our cues from culture—and fall into the trap of making value judgments on things like a child's physical features, intellectual quotient, musical talent, athletic ability, or wardrobe.

When we send our children off to school they face even more pressure to conform and perform. The educational system favors the bright child who loves to learn by studying and reading and enjoys competing for a grade. Bill remembers vividly how the students in his first-grade class knew who was really cool: the kids in the bluebird reading group. Bill's teacher put him in the robins. This was a humiliating experience because it was a slower reading group. Although Bill was (and still is!) an exceptionally intelligent person, reading never has been his strong suit, nor is it the primary way he learns.

But I can't blame cultural pressure totally for pressuring my children to perform a certain way. There was something in me that wanted to show off my child and say, "Look what I did!" I wanted everyone to know what a great mother I was, so I began to squeeze my children into my mold. For example, John endured two long years of piano lessons because I wanted him to be an excellent pianist. Evidently God didn't. John had absolutely no talent and every time I made him practice, he was totally miserable—and so was I. After I allowed him to quit, he discovered and pursued artistic abilities that he continues to enjoy and use today.

Although I still have bouts with temptation, I'm thankful God derailed me from the track of trying to make my children something besides who they are. A great debate continues to be waged over what determines who we are. Some experts argue for the environment we grew up in as the determining factor that shapes us. Others strongly believe it's our education—or lack of one. Still others say our emotional needs make us what we are. But these theories all begin from the same premise: They assume we are shapeless and blank when we arrive on the delivery table—like clay to be molded by the circumstances of life after we enter the world.

For example, maybe we think we're the way we are because our home life was difficult (or easy) when we were growing up. Perhaps life was not fair to us and we didn't get the breaks we deserved. Or maybe we were (or weren't) raised in a Christian home. Or we had a teacher who gave us a love for learning (or made us hate school).

With this mind-set, we also believe—when we become adults—we can become whatever society pressures us to be, our family needs us to be, the church recruits us to be, our friends encourage us to be, our company promotes us to be, or the state determines we should be. Certainly all of these factors influence us. However, they don't explain why we are all so different—why two children raised in the same home, by the same parents, given the same privileges, turn out so completely different.

The Bible, however, is very clear on this issue. Rather than a shapeless mass of human potential, the consistent statement of Scripture is that each one of us came with a prior design. We are not *becoming* someone—we *are* someone. Our distinctives are not the result of random selection or cultural and societal influences. We were created by a purposeful God who made us in his own image.

> Then God said, "Let us make man in our image, in our likeness, and let them rule over the fish of the sea and the birds of the air, over the livestock, over all the earth, and over all the creatures that move along the ground." (Gen. 1:26)

Furthermore, God personally designed the detailed uniqueness of every individual.

> For you created my inmost being;
>   you knit me together in my mother's womb.
> I praise you because I am fearfully and
>   wonderfully made;
>   your works are wonderful,
>   I know that full well.

> My frame was not hidden from you
>   when I was made in the secret place.
> When I was woven together in the depths of
>   the earth,
>   your eyes saw my unformed body.
> All the days ordained for me
>   were written in your book
>   before one of them came to be. (Ps. 139:13–16)

I've often marveled at the fact that there are sixty billion different fingerprints currently in use. And amazingly, we can still expect the next baby born to have ten new, totally unique prints of his or her own. How do our bodies know what to look like? A single human chromosome contains about twenty billion bits of information. This is the equivalent of about 3.3 billion characters. If the average word contains six letters, the amount of information contained in a chromosome is equivalent to 5.5 million words. If we assume there are 300 words to a page and 500 pages to a volume, then there are 3,704 volumes of information contained in one single human chromosome. Multiply that number by forty-eight chromosomes per cell and we learn that we have a staggering 177,777 volumes of information written on each cell of our bodies. Truly we are fearfully and wonderfully made. But that's only half the story.

If God goes to that much trouble with our physical body, what does this say about our complex "inmost being"—our mind, will, and emotions? Our basic strengths, abilities, and motivations are not acquired. They, too, are part of the great Designer's handiwork. What's more, nothing is arbitrary. There is purpose behind every detail. Think about what the following verses say.

For we are God's workmanship, created in Christ Jesus to do good works, which God prepared in advance for us to do. (Eph. 2:10)

> The word of the Lord came to me saying,
> "Before I formed you in the womb I knew
>   you,
> before you were born I set you apart;
> I appointed you as a prophet to the nations."
>   (Jer. 1:4, 5)

These verses make me stop in my tracks. Rather than asking who I want my children to become, I need to ask who God has made them to be already. That's not to say that they don't need to develop and mature. It simply means my children are not mine to shape. They are mine to nurture—according to their design.

If it's true that every child has a unique design, then standardized parenting is out the window. There are not "seven steps to successful parenting." Nor are there boxes or categories we can neatly fit our children into and expect to understand them. We must approach each child as the unique individual he or she is. I try to be a student of my own children—seeking to understand how they're wired so I can nurture them accordingly. I've come up with five areas critical to my understanding them.

Learning. Educators have known for years that people learn in a variety of styles. As moms, we need to understand the optimum learning situation for our children, not only to help them survive the education jungle, but to understand how to best teach them the things we want them to learn from us.

By trial and error (mostly error), I learned that John is a hands-on learner. He learns best by trying and doing, and he prefers a quiet learning environment with a mentor. He doesn't care so much about the grade he receives. Instead he wants to know whether the information he's learning is practical. Joel, on the other hand, learns by listening, memorizing, and repeating. He prefers variety in his learning environment and doesn't like to sit still for long stretches of time. His supreme goal is to make a good grade. Although James is still young, we already see that he learns best by reasoning out problems in a group setting. He does not like to study alone. Each boy approaches learning in a completely different way, and all of them make very good grades. None of these learning styles is better than the other. What's important is knowing what's most effective in motivating each child to learn.

Activities. As much as we might like to have a budding Babe Ruth or a Van Cliburn living under our roof, we need to help our children select activities that fit and complement the way they are designed. Some kids are naturally team players—so team sports make a lot of sense for them. If a child is an individualist and likes to work alone, a sport such as tennis or activities like sewing or model building might be attractive. Just be sure you don't force a child to take dancing lessons because you always wanted to be a dancer or make a child play basketball to fulfill your own dreams of being a star forward.

Discipline. If we think of discipline as a form of learning, it's easy to see why it must be tailored to the needs of the child—not the preferences of the mother. Like many moms, I started out with some definite ideas about disciplining my children. A quick swat to the seat of the pants was SOP (standard operating procedure) for John. He understood quickly he needed to change his behavior. I thought I had this discipline thing down when Joel came along four years later. Boy, was I in for a rude awakening! I might as well have given Joel a backrub if I gave him a swift swat. He needed something a little harder to get his attention. What worked for John didn't work for Joel—at all. And disciplining James is another story out of a different book. A swat on the bottom to him is tantamount to being sentenced to Alcatraz. His feelings are crushed and his self-esteem plummets. He is totally repentant about his undesirable behavior.

After nineteen years of on-the-job training, I now see that *each* situation with *each* child is a judgment call. I always try to ask myself, "What is best for *this* child in *this* situation?" But I should add a word of warning. If you decide to try this approach, be prepared to be labeled as "unfair" by older siblings if little brother or sister doesn't receive exactly the same discipline you used on them. Don't let this deter you from giving each child what he or she needs to develop his or her unique character.

Praise. Every child needs heavy doses of praise, which is something every mother can give her child. It doesn't take extra time, money, energy, or special talent. Even though giving praise is a simple thing, it's a significant thing. In dealing with my children, I try to remember these words of wisdom from Samuel Johnson: "The applause of a single human being is of great consequence."

But applause means different things to different people. It's important that we understand how each of our children likes to be applauded or praised—because each one may have a different preference. One child may feel very special when you praise him or her one-on-one in private. Whereas this may be meaningless to another child who feels special when praised in front of an audience. Still another may appreciate something tangible, such as a card or letter with a sincere message of praise. Once again we see the importance of being students of our children.

Responsibilities. I have yet to meet a child who loves to do household chores. But in most families, everyone needs to pitch in and help with cleaning and maintenance tasks. We can ease the pain of chore time by matching responsibilities with motivation. If you have a child who likes to organize, put her in charge of organizing the pantry and video cassette cabinet. Place children who like to work in teams at jobs in the same room. Set the kitchen timer for a child who likes a challenge. He'll get his chores done quickly if he knows he's in a race with the clock.

As I try to customize my mothering for each child, I try to remember my children don't need an expert; they need a guide. Because our children don't come with handling instructions, we will make mistakes. When this happens, we need to just admit them, learn from them, then get up and go on. Far from undermining our position, it will say to the child in the most powerful way, "My mom is really for me. She is on my team. She is not trying to make me something I am not."

We all ascribe to the fact that people are different—in theory. But when we have to live with the peculiarities of the people in our homes, the order of the day seems to be fix and repair, rather than accept and affirm. There will be some things about our children that annoy us. But before we get out the tool kit, we should stop and think: Is this my child's problem or mine? Is there a real problem in what my child is doing, or is he or she just not doing it my way? Is there really a perfect way to take out the garbage, clean a room, or get homework done?

No matter how good or worthy it might be, any expectation I have for my child that is motivated by my own

search of fulfillment and acceptance warps my relationship with my child. When I wrap my sense of well-being
up in my child's behavior, I am actually requiring my
child to do something for me that only God can do—make
me a whole person. As ugly as it sounds, I can easily use a
precious life that God has entrusted to my care for my
own selfish purposes. Perhaps we all need to take a careful look at what we want for our children and ask ourselves why we want it. Maybe some of us would have to
admit we need our children to be living proof of our superior mothering skills or a medium for us to be something
we always wanted to be.

Family Matters

Perhaps in the following list of Family Matters you'll
find something to think about or try with your own kids.
If you and your children are frustrated because you've
been trying to push them into a preformed mold of your
choosing, it's never too late to begin again. Become a student of your children so you can enhance their pilgrimage
to becoming what they were designed to be.

ॐ

"An unfulfilled vocation drains the colour from a man's
entire existence"—Balzac. Make note of what subjects
and activities your children enjoy so you can help them
move toward careers in which they will be fulfilled. Offer them opportunities to learn about and do things they
show interest in.

ॐ

"Don't limit a child to your own learning, for he was born
in another time"—rabbinical saying. Don't try to squeeze

a child into a mold of your own making. Be open to other possibilities.

🙊

"Happiness lies in the joy of achievement and the thrill of creative effort"—Franklin Roosevelt. What does this quote mean to you personally and in your role as a mother?

🙊

Consider how your child likes to be praised for good work or behavior. Then do it often.

🙊

Help your children set goals of what they want to learn or accomplish during the next year. Let their birthday be the beginning of their own personal year.

🙊

Take a look at the activities and sports teams your child is involved in. Do they really fit the child's abilities and desires?

🙊

"If a man is called to be a street sweeper, he should sweep streets even as Michelangelo painted, or Beethoven composed music, or Shakespeare wrote poetry. He should sweep streets so well that all the hosts of heaven and earth will pause to say, here lived a great street sweeper who did his job well"—Martin Luther King. Whatever vocations your children choose, teach them the value of doing their best job at their work.

🙊

"We can't form our children on our own concepts; we must take them and love them as God gives them to us"—

Goethe. Think about this and what it means in your family's daily life.

🍂

Evaluate how your children learn. How do they go about acquiring knowledge or skill? What environment best encourages them to learn?

🍂

"A child miseducated is a child lost"—John F. Kennedy. Don't push your child into taking courses just because they happen to be preparation for the same vocation as yours.

🍂

"Allow children to be happy in their own way, for what better way will they ever find?"— Samuel Johnson. What is your child's own way: Building? Creating? Writing? Nurturing? Teaching? Provide opportunities for your children to do the things they enjoy. On birthdays and Christmas don't buy a toy just because it's the latest thing on the market. Buy with your child's talents and abilities in mind.

🍂

Do something special to recognize a child's talent. A good friend's ten-year-old daughter wrote a fifty-page mystery book. As a surprise, the mom had the book typeset and printed to look like a real book. The daughter treasures this present.

🍂

Create a healthy balance in your children's lives to help them develop toward their full potential. Besides their schoolwork and extracurricular activities, make sure they get plenty of rest, have good eating habits, get daily exercise, have some alone time, receive spiritual input and guidance, and have time for fun and laughter.

§a.

"My business is not to remake myself, but make the absolute best of what God made"—Robert Browning. Believe this for yourself and for your children.

§a.

Don't make remarks that cause your children to feel inadequate, such as, "I thought you were smarter than that," or "Why are you acting like such a baby?"

§a.

Be a student of your child. Begin a notebook and keep a record of the things he or she loves to do. Listen to his or her thoughts. Consistency is an indication of God's design.

§a.

Concentrate on your children's strengths, and their weaknesses will become irrelevant.

§a.

"What a man thinks of himself, that it is which determines or rather indicates his fate"—Henry David Thoreau. Help your children think good things about themselves by pointing out their strengths and accomplishments.

§a.

When you are feeling honest, stop and ask yourself, Who do I need my child to be: a feather in my cap? a credit to the family name? a demonstration of my mothering skills?

the athlete or performer I never was? the popular person I never was? someone to love? someone whose needs I can meet? someone to love me? exactly what God created him or her to be?

ào

Provide space for your kids to pursue their interests and be willing to put up with some mess. Creativity usually produces chaos.

ào

Look at your child. Stop a moment and marvel at the unique creation before you. Of six billion people, you are looking at one of a kind.

ào

Start a charm bracelet for your daughter. Buy a charm to remember the special events in her life. This is a small way to show her you think her world is important.

ào

Give a son a piece of masculine jewelry, such as a ring or a cross on a gold or leather necklace to wear inside his shirt. Present it to him at a special time, and tell him it is a token of your love and belief in him.

ào

Consider how you and your child are different. What conflicts does this precipitate?

ào

Find a new way today and every day to say to your child, "You're special!" Use words and phrases such as "You're incredible," "You're a real trooper," "Magnificent!"

"Exceptional work!" "You catch on fast," "Spectacular!" "You're on target," and "You mean the world to me."

❧

"Something you consider bad may bring out your child's talents; something you consider good may stifle them"— Chateaubriand. Evaluate your personal prejudices. How do they affect your children?

3

The Self-Disciplined Child, an Endangered Species

$\mathcal{J}$ told Bill it was the sixty-fourth PTA meeting—and since it was an even number it was his turn to go. He said I was wrong. It was our sixty-seventh PTA meeting, which made it my turn not only to attend the meeting, but to drive on the next field trip. He won.

I wouldn't admit this to just anyone, but there are days I wonder if I will always have a child in elementary school. I don't remember having this much trouble with my attitude when John started school thirteen years ago. Back then I volunteered to coordinate every class outing, created fabulous charts and games to help with phonics and reading, and planned state-of-the-art craft projects. The popsicle-stick birdcage was most impressive.

I never took sides in the traditional-school/home-school controversy. I simply did both. I planned creative projects for John to work on every spare moment he was home—trying to make sure he learned something new every day. And I was the ultimate room mother at his school. Had there been a Mother of the Year Award, I would have been a top contender.

No more.

I don't know—maybe I'm just burned out. I mean how fulfilled can a woman feel trying to break the *Guinness Book of World Records* for the most crafts projects using dryer lint as a medium? And how many games of Monopoly do I have to play before the properties are condemned? And how many field trips to the penal farm can I stand before I leave the kids there and flee the country?

Perhaps, since I'm the oldest mother in the second-grade PTA, deep down I want to give younger mothers an opportunity to participate. (Well, that sounds good anyway.) If I weren't such a phony I'd tell you the young mothers probably have a lot to do with my feelings. The way I see it, why not just let these energetic, have-it-all-together women do it all?

Where *do* they get their energy? Their enthusiasm? Could I have ever really been like that? They not only show up for every meeting armed with ideas for parent projects that they'll be glad to spearhead, they seem to expect me—and every other mom and the few dads there— to willingly volunteer all our spare time for the next six months to cheerlead on their bandwagons. Or maybe they don't. Maybe I'm just feeling tired and defensive.

Or maybe I'm too busy comparing myself to some woman I'm not. I can assure you I am not thirty years old. Nor do I look like a thirty-year-old, first-time mom. This point was proven beyond a shadow of a doubt at the last end-of-school party. Trust me. You don't know depression until you're a forty-two-year-old woman chaperoning a pool party with a group of thirty-year-olds. I've always liked to be a little different and stand out in a crowd, but this wasn't what I had in mind.

In my opinion, I think swimsuit designers are one taco short of a combo plate. Do they actually believe every woman looks good wearing spandex cocktail napkins? If they were smart, they'd design swimsuits by age range, not by size, the amount of fabric commensurate with the age of the customer. I'd buy one of each color.

Truth be known, though, I wouldn't want to be a thirty-year-old mom again—bathing-suit body or not. I've realized that I can waste a lot of energy comparing myself to others. And I can spend a lot of sleepless hours in the middle of the night berating myself for not being them, for not having the time, skill, or energy to bake a cake in the shape of the entire United States big enough to feed forty second-graders to celebrate the end of their social studies unit. Or I can do the best with what I have.

I've been down this road twice before, so I understand there are areas where all children need consistent help and encouragement. I learned in the school of hard-knock motherhood—in which I have been enrolled for some time—that I've got to hang in there once more and give it my best effort for James's sake. So while all those other moms are running themselves ragged, I can put my energy where it counts—creating a warm, loving, instructive environment where he can learn to be a self-disciplined person. And the way for children to become self-disciplined is to have firm boundaries and guidelines on the outside so they're instilled on the inside.

Although it's easy to laugh at the whims or overlook the disobedient acts of young children, it is critical to remember that we need to establish limits and controls early. Otherwise, they will not learn the self-control they'll need in later years. And when the parents wait and try to lay down the law during adolescent years, the children will be more likely to react and rebel against any kind of control.

When John and Joel were young and challenged my authority, many times I wanted to brush it off and say "boys will be boys." But Bill insisted we be consistent in disciplining them. I'm thankful for his attitude. Now the boys are nineteen and fifteen, and we can relax because they learned self-discipline early.

But I have to confess, since we added a third child to our family, I find it easy to let him get away with more than his older brothers did. When John and Joel observe my lax attitude toward James, they remind me I never would have let them get away with what he does.

Just last week Joel commented pointedly, "Mom, do you realize how spoiled this child is? If I'm hungry for a snack and stand in front of the refrigerator with the door open for more than five seconds, you make me pay the electric bill. James stands there for ten minutes and you bring him a sweater."

"And please," John added sarcastically, "when we were young, we had to suffer through your ecology kick. No way would the green queen buy her children plastic toys that would end up in landfills. Frankly, Mom, I got a little tired of playing with toilet-paper tubes and left-over baked-potato foil. I was such a deprived child, you're lucky I turned out so wonderful." (It's funny how quickly teenagers can forget about their six thousand dollars' worth of electronic toys, the twenty-five-hundred-dollar computer, tennis equipment Andre Agassi only wishes he had on layaway, and their all-season Eddie Bauer wardrobe.)

Although I laugh at their comments about James having life a little easier and getting away with a little more, I think about what they're saying more than they know. Their words remind me that I need to be consistent in my philosophy of teaching self-discipline to James—even though this time around I'm older, busier, and shorter on energy. Zig Ziglar put it this way in *Raising Positive Children in a Negative World:*

> Parents, I have found out that if you are tough on yourself, life will be much easier on you. That's why it's so important for parents to train children at an early age to be self-controlled. Not to be disciplined is tantamount to disaster, because when a child gets out into the world, he will quickly discover that any discipline he has not been given by loving parents will be meted out to him by an unloving world. Developing self-control often requires painful learning experiences, but the result is well worth the effort.[1]

Helping our children become self-disciplined is one of the greatest challenges of motherhood. There are times my boys are so cooperative and self-disciplined I think they are angels on leave from heaven. Other times, when they're rebelliously expressing their self-will, I feel like grabbing the first blunt object and using it on their south end. I don't have to look far to find evidence that all of us "have sinned and fall short of the glory of God" (Rom. 3:23). But sad to say, my own behavior and attitudes remind me frequently it's easier to sin than to do what is right.

I see this struggle in my children as well. Every child is born with this natural commitment to self-centered behavior. When the boys were young, I marveled at how adept they were at lying. I wanted to have precocious children, but practicing the art of deception a year before parenting books predicted they would was not what I envisioned.

I'm thankful to be able to say my boys are wonderful guys, and they each know the value of telling the truth.

But they've had to learn it. And there were times when the learning was painful—for them and for me. This learning process is called discipline.

Discipline is actually a lifelong process under God's direction. As the divine parent, God undertakes the challenge of teaching his children the truth about the consequences of self-centered living.

> My son, do not regard lightly the discipline of
>   the LORD,
> nor faint when you are reproved by Him. . . .
> It is for discipline that you endure; God deals
> with you as with sons; for what son is there whom his
> father does not discipline? (Heb. 12:5–8 NASB)

The Bible clearly indicates that God delegates this responsibility to me, the parent, to discipline my children when they are young. "Don't fail to correct your children; discipline won't hurt them! They won't die if you use a stick on them! Punishment will keep them out of hell" (Prov. 23:13–14 TLB). This is obviously a part of motherhood God does not intend for me to take lightly.

I've found it helpful to remember discipline is both a *process* and a *product*. "Do not regard lightly the discipline [process] of the LORD. . . . It is for discipline [product] that you endure." Discipline always has a goal. It is not simply the changing or controlling of my child's behavior, but helping my child change his mind and character. There's something bigger going on here than just teaching him not to say he ate two cookies if he really ate five.

Every one of us was born with a basic belief that we can find fulfillment in this world apart from God. That's part of the human condition. This includes my children. Proverbs 22:15 reminds me, "Folly is bound up in the heart of a child, / but the rod of discipline will drive it far from him."

But I don't want you to think the Bible advocates we keep a big stick holstered at our side! The apostle Paul gives wise advice to fathers (and mothers too, I think) in Ephesians 6:4: "Fathers, do not exasperate your children; instead, bring them up in the training and instruction of the Lord."

A wise older mother of four wonderful children gave me some advice when my first child was born. She said, "Kathy, remember: A mother must be fun-loving so her children will enjoy her presence, but she must also stand firm and be fair. Don't let your children walk all over you—lest they lose their respect for you."

She also suggested I treat my young children the same way God treated his children at Mount Sinai when they were still immature in their relationship with him and in their knowledge of life. When God gave his children his rules, the Ten Commandments, he didn't explain *why* they shouldn't commit murder or adultery, he just told them *not to do it*. They were to trust in his authority and trust that he knew what was best for them. In the same way, I shouldn't rationalize and explain to an eighteen-month-old why he can't run out into the street. He needs to understand that he doesn't run out into the street because I said not to—and that's that.

Yet in dealing with older children, we should be careful not to frustrate them by answering "because I say so" indiscriminately. When dealing with teenagers, it's important to not only teach them good behavior, but why good behavior is important. Sometimes I think we use the "because I'm the mother" reason out of pure laziness and sometimes out of frustration, knowing our kids are trying to wear us down. Granting or refusing permission should be an opportunity for communication and instruction. And that takes time, commitment, and energy on our part.

I thought about my mentor's advice and set a goal to be a mother who was fair, firm, and fun. That was nineteen years ago. I will say that the fairness and firmness have paid off—and so has the fun. I would start over again today using the same three objectives as guidelines.

Be fair. My authority is not unbridled. As a mother, I am strictly working as God's agent and under his authority. When I become unreasonable in my demands or if I discipline my children in anger, *I* am the one who needs the discipline. God requires me to be both fair and appropriate.

But in order to be fair, it's extremely important to discover why the child is misbehaving—*before* I select the appropriate disciplinary response. More than a few times I have gone ballistic in irritation over something one of the boys has done. Just last week was case in point.

I strive to be reasonably responsible about nutrition. I try to make sure the kids eat a well-balanced diet. This does *not* mean because one loaf of my homemade bread weighs the same as a two-liter bottle of cola, they can choose the cola.

In my opinion, good nutrition means if they want to enjoy some junk food, they'd best take their vitamins and eat what's good for them as well. Last week James did not seem to be cooperating with the rule.

When the rest of the family had finished their dinner, I noticed James was fooling around with the vegetables on his plate. In an impatient voice, I told him he had ten minutes to eat his dinner, or he would be disciplined. We left him alone at the table.

Ten minutes later, I came back into the room and saw the same green beans still on his plate. I hit the ceiling.

When big tears started rolling down his cheeks, I thought he was trying to make me feel sorry for him because he didn't like what I had fixed.

On the way from the table to his bedroom for discipline, I noticed his arm felt warm. I felt his forehead and realized he had a fever. Small wonder he didn't want to eat; he was sick. After apologizing, I wondered if I would ever learn to respond wisely and not react rashly to my children's apparent acts of disobedience.

In nineteen years of motherhood, I've discovered and recorded at least five reasons why children disobey and violate my expectations. I strive to remember that each reason demands an appropriate, fair response.

They don't understand. Sometimes a child simply does not know he or she did something wrong. This can stem from either our failure to communicate or the child's ability to comprehend. If this is the case, the child needs clarification of the issue—not punishment. Especially with a young child, a fair response is to ask, "Did you understand you were not supposed to . . . ?"

They didn't remember. Sometimes children forget because they don't take us seriously, but honest memory lapses should be handled as such. This is a constant problem with younger children. Sometimes it helps to give a child a reminder *and* a warning concerning the consequences of regular forgetfulness. When our boys were younger, a quick glance at "Mr. Helper," a wooden spoon we used in discipline, was all it took to help them remember something next time.

They are not capable. Sometimes children are either physically, mentally, or emotionally incapable of following the rules. A chronic problem of many parents is having unrealistic expectations of younger children. We can't seem to understand why they can't sit through a two-hour concert, keep their clothes spotless, or keep from spilling their milk.

As a young pastor's wife, I expected our boys to be the model of decorum, sitting quietly in church like adults. Bad idea. A tired, hungry three-year-old will misbehave, not because he is rebellious, but because he is not mature enough to act differently than he feels. Milk will be spilt, not because a five-year-old is being careless, but because his hands are small and uncoordinated. Before I react harshly to apparent misbehavior, I need to stop and ask myself if my expectations are appropriate to the child's capability to respond. It's not fair to ask children to behave beyond their years.

They may not trust us. There can be a vast difference in a child's perspective and a parent's perspective of a problem. For example, I've been through some big battles trying to get splinters out of fingers. I'll never forget the day I was getting madder by the minute because I thought John was just being stubborn about a little splinter. I might as well have been speaking Swahili when I said, "Sit still. This won't hurt." His crying escalated to screaming and his wiggling to writhing. I calmed down when I realized getting a splinter out with a needle was as traumatic to a five-year-old as minor surgery was to me. He didn't know that he would feel better once the splinter was out. He had no basis to trust me because instead of listening to his fears I told him he was making a mountain out of a molehill. Sometimes molehills are mountains from a child's perspective.

Children need our understanding. Being fair means showering compassion and tenderness about the things that are big deals to them. Then they will be more likely to trust us in other matters.

They simply may want their own way. Much misbehavior simply comes down to a battle of the wills. When a child thinks *I'm going to do what I want to do when I want to do it*, fair and appropriate discipline is the only answer.

Be firm. Discipline should be carried out in a context of love and tenderness. Our children need to know that we're not disciplining them because we're tired, cranky, or mean people. They need to know, always, that we love them and that we want what's best for them. When my response to a child is based on my frustration rather than on what's best for him or her, I can be sure I'm off track. Whenever I find myself getting agitated at one of the boys, I need to stop and ask myself what's going on. Is this my problem or his?

I have to be especially careful about how I respond to my children at "that time of the month." When I have PMS, it's easy for my perspective to get out of whack. I'm tempted to react to something one of the boys did, rather than respond in wisdom. I've found one of the most important disciplines in my own life is to keep my mouth shut when I'm not completely sure about the issues and I don't feel in control of my emotions. Unrestrained words can wound deeply. In Edith Schaeffer's book *What Is a Family?* she wrote about the destructive power of words. They are indelibly etched in my mind.

> One lesson I tried to teach my children from an early age, repeating over and over again the best explanation I could think of, in different ways at different times, was the fact that some things must never be said, no matter how hot the argument, no matter how angry one becomes, no matter how far one goes in feeling, "I don't care how much I hurt him [or her]." Some things are too much of a "luxury" *ever* to say. Some things are too great a price to pay for the momentary satisfaction of cutting the other person down. Some things are like throwing indelible ink on

a costly work of art, or smashing a priceless statue just to make a strong point in an argument. Saying certain things is an expense beyond reason. This is true for man, woman, and child.[2]

If we say to a child, in so many words, "You are a dumb or insensitive or uncaring person because you hit your sister rather than talking about your problems . . ." or if we imply by our actions (or reactions) that the child is dumb for having done something, we are using hurtful words and we are not disciplining in a loving and tender context. It is very important to distinguish between the person and the behavior when we discipline a child. We do not want to give the message that he or she is a bad person. We do want to give the message that hitting in anger, or whatever, is not the way a loving, caring person handles problems.

Discipline must always go hand-in-hand with instruction. I try hard to remember that the goal is to change the way my child *thinks* so he can—in turn—change his own behavior. Discipline is a lot more than the ability to skillfully wield the paddle. In fact there are at least five avenues or forms of discipline found in the Bible every mother needs to use.

Instruction: Preventive Discipline. It is my job as a mother to communicate God's truth to the next generation. In a world filled with relativistic thinking, our kids need to know that there is such a thing as right and wrong. They need to know what is good—the things that delight the heart of God. They need to know what is bad—the things that displease their Maker. And they need to have clear limits that are consistent with God's Word. As a mom, I can't delegate this responsibility to someone else. Without a doubt, the home is the most important classroom. Whether it's through reading a Bible story and talking about how it applies to everyday life or stopping in the middle of a difficult circumstance to talk about how God would want us to respond, my children need to hear the truth from me.

Modeling: Illustrated Discipline. Like it or not, my boys are constantly watching Bill and me to see if what we say is really true. Certainly more is caught than taught. That's why Moses commanded the Israelites,

> Hear, O Israel: The LORD our God, the LORD is one. Love the LORD your God with all your heart and with all your soul and with all your strength. These commandments that I give you today are to be upon your hearts. Impress them on your children. Talk about them when you sit at home and when you walk by the road, when you lie down and when you get up. Tie them as symbols on your hands and bind them on your foreheads. Write them on the doorframes of your houses and on your gates. (Deut. 6:4–9)

Children need to see truth being lived out before their eyes. That's what attaching commands to hands, foreheads, and doors is all about. The Israelites took this mandate literally and actually attached phylacteries, little boxes with passages of Scripture inside, to their foreheads. But I think what God is really saying here is that he wants his truth to permeate every area of our lives: through our hands—what we do and how we work; through our heads—how we think and use our minds; in our houses—how we live behind closed doors; and in the gates—how we govern ourselves and conduct business.

Guidance: Corrective Discipline. Since I travel frequently, I spend a lot more time in airplanes than I care to.

It gives me comfort to know there are very proficient individuals at the controls of highly technical instruments following a reliable flight plan. But more than once we have made a mid-course correction to avoid a thunderstorm or adjust for cross winds.

All of us need correction in life as well. The cross winds of culture coupled with our internal sinfulness blow us off the course God intends for us to travel. Part of our function as mothers is to warn our children when they start to get off course.

One of the saddest passages in the Bible speaks of a father's failure to rebuke his children. I think we can learn some things about mothering from it also. "For I have told him [Eli] that I am about to judge his house forever for the iniquity which he knew, because his sons brought a curse on themselves and he did not rebuke them" (1 Sam. 3:13 NASB).

A rebuke has a very simple purpose: to protect the child from the consequences of continuing in his present course. A rebuke is not to humiliate the child, but to encourage. It is not to demonstrate mother's authority, but to call on the child's internal character to change. A rebuke is a word of warning that does three things. It makes the child aware of his error. It clarifies the consequences for the error. And it outlines the desired alternatives: "James, we don't call each other stupid. You know that, and I will have to punish you if you do it again. If you have a problem with your brother, ask him politely to stop bothering you. If he doesn't cooperate come see me; but you may not call him stupid."

Reward: Persuasive Discipline. Every mother needs to understand a very basic law that God built into every human being: Behavior that achieves desirable results will be repeated. Obviously, God understands this and makes the rewards for walking in his ways very clear in the Bible. Of course our children need to learn to do the right thing because it's the right thing to do. But rewards can make learning fun and can give the child pleasure—which reinforces good behavior and attitudes. Unfortunately, the law of reinforcement can work against us, as well, by reinforcing poor behavior. If I reward a temper tantrum with the attention a child is otherwise not getting, I can be sure I'll see more of the same.

Most of the time we think of rewards as money, candy, or gifts of some sort. But rewards do not have to be material in nature. A well-timed word of praise calculated to touch what your child really values is one of the sweetest rewards he will receive on earth.

Another type of reward is privilege. Since John got his driver's license three years ago, he has been very responsible about letting us know where he is and what time he'll be home. Right now he is planning a ski trip for a group of senior guys—to take by themselves. We are happy to give him this privilege and to help him pay for the trip as a reward for his trustworthiness.

But it's important to remember rewards are no substitute for authority. Never use rewards as a bribe. The goal of discipline is to produce a disciplined person. You want to reward discipline. If you bribe for good behavior, you are reinforcing irresponsibility.

Punishment: Punitive Discipline. In my book the mom who enjoys punishing her child doesn't have both oars in the water. But the time comes for every mother, after instructions have been clearly given and warnings have been made, when negative reinforcement must be brought to bear. Retribution has nothing to do with it. Anger has no place in it. The goal of punishment is to teach the child that self-centered behavior leads to pain and emptiness.

Controlled punishment and denial of certain privileges that teach this principle without harming the child physically or emotionally are important tools of discipline. A mother needs four things to be successful with this type of discipline.

First, she needs a compassionate heart. I have found a time of discipline can be a warm and tender time if I make sure my sense of frustration does not break the love bond. It's of utmost importance that I take time to talk about the reason for punishment and why this is happening and remind the child of my love.

I should never mete out punishment in the heat of the moment. Anger must be controlled. The anger of a woman does not achieve the righteousness of God in her children. Talk things over with your husband if appropriate. Above all, talk things over with God. James 1:5 is the mother's life verse: "If any of you lacks wisdom, he should ask God."

Second, she needs a listening ear. It is important to take time to listen with focused concern to really understand the child's point of view. Whether you agree or disagree, make sure your child knows you are listening.

Third, she needs a determined courage. There is, in a sense, a dark side of love that refuses to let a person take a path of destruction. I try to think about the big pain in the future this small pain will help my child avoid.

And fourth, she needs wise judgment. It's important to make sure the punishment is appropriate to the offense and that it is realistic. When a friend caught her son sneaking out of the house to meet his friends late at night, she grounded him for the next nine months from going anyplace with any of his friends. Nine months is a *long* time. The sentence lasted about two weeks. This incident occurred four years ago. Since then there have been more instances where the mom did not follow through on what she said. I'm sad to say the son's respect for his mother's authority has diminished significantly.

Be fun. Strange as it seems, having fun with your children has a great deal to do with how they respond to your firmness. The moments you spend laughing, playing, and enjoying life together make large deposits in your child's emotional bank account. They understand your love and commitment to them in tangible ways. So when the time comes to be firm and administer discipline, their account is sufficient to stand a withdrawal.

I've met more than a few frustrated mothers who have forgotten how to have fun. The circumstances of life have hardened their personalities, and they now take life, as well as themselves, too seriously. This kind of attitude isn't healthy for anyone.

Learning to be a fun person means being willing to lighten up, laugh at yourself, and enjoy life. You'd be surprised at the seemingly adverse circumstances that, when seen through a different lens, can really be funny. Even bringing humor into some disciplinary situations can take the edge off a tense situation. It is possible to laugh about the situation and be serious about the behavior.

To me, wise discipline is one of the toughest parts of motherhood—so I'm always on a sharp learning curve. I like what Tom Landry said about discipline. Although he comes from the context of football, I find a lot of truth in his words for mothers too.

> Most successful players not only accept rules and limitations, I believe they need them. In fact, I believe players are free to perform at their best only when they know what the expectations are, where the limits stand.

I see this as a biblical principle that also applies to life, a principle our society as a whole has forgotten: you can't enjoy true freedom without limits.

We often resent rules because they limit what we can do. Yet without the rules that define a football game, you can't play the game, let alone enjoy it. The same thing is true in life. To live and enjoy the freedom we have in America, we have to live by the rules of society. To live life to its fullest and truly enjoy it, we need to understand and abide by the rules God spells out in the Bible. God isn't out to spoil our fun; he knows that life without limits results in anarchy and misery. It's only when we have absolute limits that we can be truly free to enjoy the best life has to offer.[3]

Raising our children in an environment of fair and firm discipline with definite limitations and guidelines doesn't ensure they will learn self-discipline, but lack of discipline and definite limitations pretty much ensures they won't be self-disciplined.

Family Matters

Maybe you feel your children—not to mention you, yourself—are frustrated because the limits and rules have not been clear. Perhaps their behavior has gotten out of hand and so has your temper. Or perhaps you're not at the point where things are out of control. But maybe you're looking for some ways to help your children acquire a sense of self-discipline. Today could be a turning point in your family. Think about the following ideas and act upon one or two you feel might help your kids.

§&

"Our chief want in life is somebody who will make us do what we can"—Ralph Waldo Emerson. Remember, when you must inflict a little pain in the short run, you are paving the way for your child to be successful and self-disciplined in the long run.

ॐ

Studies show that average parents spend only twenty minutes a day communicating with their children, and nine of those minutes are spent in disciplinary situations. Try to disprove this study in your family.

ॐ

"Who, then, is free? The man who can govern himself"— Horace. When you are disciplining your children, remember the goal of discipline is self-discipline. Try to find ways to "tell" them this both through discipline and with words. For example, if your teenager loses a notebook in a messy room, you might talk about the consequences of not being self-disciplined enough to keep track of important papers. The consequences might include explaining the loss to a teacher, cleaning the room on Friday night instead of going out, and working with you to set up an organized space for important things like homework.

ॐ

Honestly examine your own life. Are there areas where you are knowingly not setting a good example for your children? If so, you will probably find it difficult to discipline your children in these areas. Lead a life of self-discipline yourself.

ॐ

Keep your children's emotional tank full. Regularly do something fun together. Sitting in front of the television together doesn't count. Try something out of the ordinary—

learn to rollerblade, conquer a computer program, invent a new cookie recipe, plan a trip.

ৰ৹

Buy a copy of *The New Dare to Discipline* by Dr. James Dobson (Tyndale, 1992) and use it with your young children.

ৰ৹

Stop and think when you're tempted to scream "Because I said so!" Wield your authority carefully.

ৰ৹

Remember, our children will respect us more if we are not afraid to set standards. Being a mother is not a popularity contest. Respect, like trust, must be earned.

ৰ৹

In his book, *To Resist or Surrender,* psychologist Paul Tournier wrote, "There are many parents who do not want to argue with their children over every mistake. They reserve their authority for serious matters, but then it is too late." Perhaps the toughest judgment call a mother must make is in choosing her battles. Ask God to help you know which ones to fight.

ৰ৹

"There are two ways of exerting one's strength: One is pushing down, the other is pulling up"—Booker T. Washington. How do you exert strength? Make an ongoing list of ways you could help pull your children up. Refer to it often.

ৰ৹

Read the book of Proverbs. Teach these principles for wise living to your children and apply them to your own life as well. There are thirty-one chapters in Proverbs, one for each day of the month, each full of the wisdom we need to be good mothers.

❧

Ask yourself this question about your child's behaviors: What am I laughing at today that I do not want to see repeated when my child gets older?

❧

Remember: You are God's agent in teaching your child self-control. This means you should stop regularly and ask yourself, "What would Jesus do in this situation?"

❧

All of us lose our tempers at times. When this happens, ask for forgiveness and move on. Don't wallow in your guilt. Don't abdicate your responsibility just because you make mistakes periodically.

❧

Always stop and ask why before you act: Did he understand what was the right thing to do? Did she forget? Is he capable of doing what you expected of him? Does she trust you? Is he being stubborn and self-willed?

❧

Read Ross Campbell's books *How to Really Love Your Child* (Victor Books, 1977), and *How to Really Love Your Teenager* (Victor Books, 1981).

❧

Take a look at the five avenues of discipline: instruction, modeling, guidance, reward, and punishment. Where are you the strongest? Weakest? What works best with each child?

ॐ

God's first commandment with a promise is, "Honor your father and your mother, so that you may live long in the land the LORD your God is giving you" (Exod. 20:12). If I want my children to honor me, I need to model this behavior by honoring my own parents.

ॐ

"Raised voices lower esteem. Hot tempers cool friendships. Loose tongues stretch truth. Swelled heads shrink influence. Sharp words dull respect"—William A. Ward. What do these words mean to you?

ॐ

"Discipline is the soul of an army. It makes small numbers formidable, procures success to the weak, and esteem to all"—George Washington. Don't be afraid to discipline your children. Done properly, it's for their good.

ॐ

Read *Raising Positive Kids in a Negative World* by Zig Ziglar (Oliver Nelson, 1985).

4

The Official Referee's Guide for Sibling Combat

C/I think it was either Moses—or Charlton Heston—who said, "Lord, send someone else to do it." When it comes to teaching kids to get along, this is my prayer as well. I *do not* like playing referee. But I believe it's important for kids to learn how to get along in the world, which means they must first learn to get along with each other.

Some child-raising experts say there is such a thing as compliant siblings—brothers and sisters who play peacefully together for hours at a time. Don't you believe a word of it. Call it a mother's intuition, but I knew we were in for trouble when I found a copy of *The Battle Secrets of Attila the Hun* hidden between books two and three of *The Chronicles of Narnia*.

If I didn't know better, I would swear my children studied sibling combat techniques in school. The course descriptions read something like this:

Torture: How to Make Younger Siblings See Things Your Way. Learn the art of pinching, pulling hair, and scratching moles off so as to draw blood. Special attention is given to precision tripping, squeezing, and kicking. Mats furnished.

Creative Tattling 101. Master the talent of effectively tattling in response to mandates such as "nanny-nanny-boo-boo, stick your head in doo-doo." Find out how to get your mother's sympathy when your brother threatens to shoot your lips off and put them in a box. Learn how to communicate your feelings using volume, pitch, and tears. Class size limited.

Seminar in Name-calling. Learn from experts how the power of words can devastate your enemy. More than one thousand names guaranteed to hurt feelings. An analysis of how to target appropriate terms with corresponding character traits for maximum results. Special attention given to making others feel fat, stupid, and useless. Enrollment limited to those who have taken "Advanced Four-Letter Words."

How to Be Selfish: Your Rights. Know the law. Are you required to share your belongings with brothers and sisters? Can you sue if your toys are used without permission? Are parental rules binding? Learn loopholes from a panel of legal experts to help you always be first and get your way in everything.

Most mothers instinctively know that when a child is old enough to use his little sister as a dartboard he is ready to learn some manners, to understand every person is worthy of respect, and to practice some basic principles about getting along in the human race. I'm of the opinion these attitudes and behaviors must be learned at home in the context of the family before they'll be carried out on the playground or football field.

This means getting a handle on sibling rivalry.

Good luck.

Every mother understands there will be ongoing sibling disputes that she must control—or go bonkers. Verbal and sometimes physical battles are often precipitated by personality clashes, a child's lack of maturity to see things from another's point of view, or volatile circumstances. I identified the major hot spots that caused contention between our kids and try to avoid these situations like the plague. Of course, they have to continue eating at the same dinner table and riding in the car at the same time, but there are some circumstances I can control.

For years I avoided buying a home video-game system. The times we rented a system for the weekend, I saw what it did to my children. They became possessed. If one boy didn't get to play the exact number of milliseconds as another, he wanted to see his brother's body outlined in chalk. And heaven forbid someone's turn was skipped. You'd think he'd lost his birthright.

Actually, it was only after our children applied for admittance to Boys Town that we bought a video-game system. Since then, I've come to the conclusion that video games were invented in hell. When the children play, it's virtually impossible to pry them away—short of threatening to quarantine our home from the pizza delivery man. Every once in a while one of the boys will turn off a game on first request, but it's usually because he hasn't taken a bathroom break in three hours.

I put my foot down when one boy accidentally blocked the television screen, causing his brother to scream bloody murder and sink into deep depression because now Prince Vexkorg, ruler of Gurflotch, couldn't conquer King Zordash, lord of Sweenunu. I decided this probably wasn't optimum behavior, and it had to stop.

Like many kids, ours have had to learn how to control their feelings and treat others with respect or incur the wrath of their mother—which is no picnic. They've had to share bedrooms, bathrooms, toys, clothes, and athletic equipment. Since we could not afford one of everything for everybody, much less psychiatric care for me, we decided to work hard on learning to get along. This meant formulating some relational and behavioral guidelines to teach the kids—and to live by as a family. We also relieved a lot of bickering when we set up simple systems so each child received his fair share of privileges and responsibilities.

Today, our kids are nineteen, fifteen, and eight, and they've come a long way. Although the jury is still out as far as how our kids will turn out in the long run, this past Thanksgiving our children were the primary focus of our thankfulness.

We spent the holiday with the our long-time friends Bill and Judie Byrd and some of their relatives. At the end of the feast, our host commented that the past year had been a hard year for many people and that when times are hard, we find out who our friends really are. He asked each of us to think of a friend for whom we were thankful—someone who had stuck with us during the rough spots of life—and share, in turn, about why we were thankful for that friend.

The stories were touching as each person described sincere appreciation for someone who had stood by his or her side. On Joel's turn, he surprised us all by giving a short speech about how thankful he was for his big brother. He shared how John helped him acclimate to high school and let him hang around with his senior friends. Joel said he was grateful to have a big brother who treated him with kindness and patience, and whose life was a model to follow. When he sat down, there were few dry eyes in the room. Everyone was well aware that teenage brothers—especially those who have to share every-thing—usually don't like each other.

That night my husband Bill and I were lying awake in bed with the lights off, overwhelmed with having such incredible kids. Of course, they're not perfect—and nei-ther are we. But it is an indescribable blessing to be a part of a family of people who like each other, enjoy being to-gether, and get along most of the time.

When people quiz us about why our kids get along so well, we're quick to respond we feel it is because of God's grace. We've made—and continue to make—a lot of mis-takes. But I think two things have helped. First, we believe mutual respect is one of the most important ingredients in a healthy family. Children should be taught from an early age to treat each other with courtesy and not to take oth-ers for granted. We make a big deal about manners at our house. Teaching children common courtesies, social disci-plines, and table manners will build their self-image and help them get along with each other, as well as the rest of the world.

Second, having a set of family house rules has made a big difference. When the boys were younger, Bill and I wrote these rules for our family. Then we read them to the boys and explained we would all strive to live up to these standards.

House Rules

Rule 1. We're all in this together. The rules apply to everyone—even Mom and Dad. One of the first things I learned about mothering is that kids won't buy a double standard. It's important that children understand the rules apply to *everyone* in the house—no exceptions. When you

give them permission to call you on the carpet for a violation they will feel ownership of the rules. Albert
Schweitzer said, "Example isn't the most important thing,
example is the only thing." We must practice what we
preach.

Also, if your children aren't getting along, you might
want to ask yourself what kind of relational roles you're
setting. Do you and your husband treat each other with
courtesy and respect? Or do you raise your voices and
make unkind, cutting remarks to each other?

I have a friend whose children were behaving rudely
and disrespectfully toward each other. This friend asked
me one day if I had any suggestions to help her kids learn
to treat each other nicely—they were driving her nuts! (I
had visited her home and I totally understood why!) In the
course of the conversation I learned she and her husband
were in the habit of making sarcastic, disrespectful remarks at each other. She answered her own question and
later asked her husband if they could agree to stop their
own childish behavior. In a family meeting they confessed
their less-than-optimum example to the kids. With their
relationship setting the pace, they made a family decision
to treat each other with courtesy. Five years later I can
honestly report their home is a delightful place.

Rule 2. No yelling at anyone. In our home we reserve
yelling and screaming for emergencies only. Authority
does not increase with volume. We laid down the rule
about yelling and we enforce the consequences. "Outside
voices" are not to be used inside, and yelling at others is
not tolerated. Remember, the moment you are drawn into
a yelling match, you surrender parental authority to the
strength of the personalities involved. When I find myself
tempted to raise my voice in a show of authority, I try to

think of something Margaret Thatcher said: "Being powerful is like being a lady. If you have to tell people you are, you aren't." If I have to raise my voice to prove I'm in authority, then I'm not.

When we are emotionally wound up, our voices magnify. Be aware of this when dealing with a problem. Slow down your own speech. This will help you speak in a more gentle tone of voice.

If you're hot and you aren't sure you can control your feelings, get away for a few minutes to regroup. If you can't get away, force yourself to count to one hundred slowly. Once *you've* calmed down, you can lay down the law with the kids about talking things over calmly.

If you sense your children becoming louder and more violent in their behavior, you might evaluate what they're watching on television. In a report from the American Academy of Pediatrics, pediatricians concluded that repeated exposure to television violence can make children not only accepting of real-life violence, but more violent themselves.

Rule 3. Delete the phrase "Shut up!" from our vocabulary entirely. Every human being is a worthwhile, uniquely made individual, worthy of respect. Don't tolerate these or any other disrespectful or devaluing words between family members. Make sure everyone knows there will be consequences for offenders.

When our kids get on each other's nerves, or when someone interrupts a conversation, they are allowed to say, "Please be quiet." Since kids will be kids and sometimes don't want to comply with the requests of a sibling, if the offender does not voluntarily refrain from talking by the third request, a judge (usually a parent) is brought in and we sit down and talk about what's going on. Many times the behavior is just to annoy the brother who's asking for silence. In this case, I deal with the annoying behavior and talk to the offender about the importance of showing preference to others above ourselves.

Rule 4. Calling names or making unkind, cutting remarks to each other is strictly out of order. There's an old saying: "To belittle is to be little." Talk to your children about the meaning of this saying. Help them understand that you're being a small person if you find it necessary to cut someone else down.

In our family we do a lot of kidding and joking. My kids will grow up remembering teasing me about my cooking and remedial domestic abilities as one of their most cherished family traditions. Telling blonde jokes is also one of their favorite pastimes. Just yesterday they approached me in the kitchen. John faked a sincere look on his face and asked:

"Mom, do you know how to drown a blonde?"

"No, and I'm sure I won't continue to breathe unless you tell me," I responded with a smirk.

"Tape a mirror to the bottom of the pool!" They laughed and prepared for round two.

"Here's an easy one for you," Joel continued. "What do you call ten blondes standing in a circle?"

"I give," I sighed and played along.

"A dope ring," he spurted out while they both went into hysteria.

The fact that we laugh a lot with and at each other is one of the things I enjoy most about our family. But every family must have boundaries. Some comments are definitely out of bounds and do not fall into the category of playful teasing. It's important that when family members poke fun at one another, it's fun for everyone. It's not funny to joke about someone's big nose, deformities, seemingly stupid mistakes, fears, or weaknesses. If feelings are hurt over a comment made in a joking manner, be sure to talk it out so it won't happen again.

Rule 5. Work out potential problems ahead of time. At one point in our family life, "It's your turn" and "I did it last time" arguments were causing me to give my kids a piece of my mind—that I couldn't afford to lose. We were all wasting precious emotional energy over small issues. To combat the problem, we decided at a family meeting to set up a chore system so each child knew exactly whose responsibility it was to do what. This has worked well for a number of years. Now, John always cleans the kitchen on Mondays, Wednesdays, and Fridays. Joel takes Tuesdays, Thursdays, and Saturdays. James knows it's his job to feed the dogs and haul the empty garage cans back from the street. No questions asked.

I was also growing weary of the kids bickering in the car over who sat where and which tape we'd listen to. We all agreed on a fair way to rotate privileges. Now, we rotate monthly (or weekly) who gets to ride "shotgun" in the car. This person also gets to choose which cassette tape to play first. This decision has been made ahead of time—so now they can find something else to pick at each other about.

Rule 6. Keep confidential what we share with each other. Your children need to know they can trust you. Don't talk about one child's problems to another child. And don't talk to your friends about confidential matters your child shares with you.

One mother virtually ruined her own daughter's reputation and their relationship by openly talking to other mothers about how she couldn't trust her daughter. Although the daughter had only abused her mother's trust once by sneaking out with an older boy before her parents would let her date, when the news traveled—as it unfortunately does—the occurrence was blown way out of proportion in the minds of those who heard the rumor. The mother and the daughter are now estranged.

In another instance a very wise mother learned her teenage son had been drinking. They openly talked about this and dealt with his behavior firmly, but lovingly, in the privacy of their family. Although he made some bad choices, today this boy has a shining reputation and a wonderful relationship with his parents.

Rule 7. Take responsibility for our own actions and words. Children need help learning how to work through conflicts. They don't know how to do this instinctively. When they're fighting, sit them down and hear both sides of the story. Ask them questions that make each one think about both sides of the problem. Guide them to discover what the root problem really is and focus on their behavior—not what was done to them.

Help your children learn the principle that small people blame others for their mistakes and actions. Make them aware of the fact that they are always responsible for their own actions and that you hold them responsible for their actions—no matter what the other person does. There is no excuse for poor behavior, a poor response, or blaming someone else for our problems.

But if I want my kids to live by this principle, that means I need to live by it also—no matter what the circumstance. Recently the older boys became aware of a situation in my business where someone had not fulfilled an obligation and left me in a very difficult situation that had far-reaching effects. I knew they were watching to see how I would respond. Although I have to confess I entertained thoughts of blame and getting even, having this house rule for our family reminded me of the importance of responding wisely.

Rule 8. Ask forgiveness when we have hurt or offended someone, even if it was an accident. Sometimes it's hard for kids to see the importance of restoring a relationship—especially if they can't see they did anything wrong. It's important that we teach them to try to feel the other person's pain or discomfort. Make sure you set the example by apologizing when you hurt or disappoint them—even if it was unintentional. Saying "I'm sorry" or "I was wrong" won't undermine your authority. Living a double standard will.

For women like me who do daily battle with pride, these little words are very hard to get off the tip of my tongue, but I'm making progress—slowly but surely. Bill has been a wonderful example to me by the way he sincerely asks forgiveness when one of the kids or I feel offended.

Rule 9. Respect each other's space. Everyone needs a degree of privacy. We make a habit of always knocking before opening someone's closed door. All children need to have a sense of ownership and privacy. They need a place where they can daydream, try on clothes, experiment with makeup, practice shaving, and lie down quietly after a demanding day at school. Talk openly about giving each other space and respecting each other's feelings.

In our family, our teenagers share a room. They've learned to give each other privacy when needed. And since one of the boys is a creative slob (to put it mildly), and the other one likes order and neatness, they've had to learn to think of each other's feelings and cut each other slack in this area as well.

When a family lives together in restricted space, it's important for everyone to be aware that sound travels and what a person does in one room affects others in a room nearby. This means when the boys turn on their CD player, they recognize that I'm down the hall trying to concentrate on writing a chapter. It also means when Mom and Dad turn on the television on a school night, they realize the noise can be annoying or distracting to a student trying to study for a test.

Rule 10. Respect each other's stuff. I am amazed at the way some children mistreat the property of others. We've had guests break toys, appliances, and furniture—without even so much as an "I'm sorry" from the child—and sometimes the parents. One afternoon a neighborhood child broke a brand-new twenty-dollar toy James had saved his money for and bought that morning. Without even a word of apology, the child just left and didn't come back for two weeks.

We all want our children to learn to respect the property of others and to share their belongings with others. To do this they must have a sense of control over their things and respect the control someone else has over their things. This means if James has a friend over and they want to play with something that belongs to a big brother who isn't home to give his permission, then they find something else to play with. It means if Joel wants to wear a sweater of John's, he asks John first. It also means I respect their property as well.

When we moved into our present house, I enjoyed decorating each room and creating a warm and attractive atmosphere. I started to work on the teenagers' room one day when they were at school. When they returned home, they gasped when I threatened to take their cola-can sculpture out of their window. "Mom, this is creative!" Creative, yes. Attractive, no. But in a rare moment of strength, I realized that it's more important for them to create their own teenager-friendly environment they'll enjoy than for me to win the House Beautiful Award. And redoing their things without their approval would have been a violation of their privacy. Although I'm sure their cola-can window treatment will never be featured in a decorator magazine, I'm just thankful it's not beer cans.

Creating your own set of house rules to help you maintain some semblance of order can save a lot of emotional energy that would have been used to fuss and argue. But there are long-term benefits also. The relational skills your kids learn at home—respecting others' feelings and their property—will it make it easier for them to form healthy relationships with friends, college roommates, their spouse, co-workers, and associates in the future.

Family Matters

It's important when we think about teaching our children to get along that we ask ourselves if we're adding to the problem. Have we been playing favorites or unconsciously ignoring a less-demanding child? Do we expect our children to do everything together? Are there unhealthy communication habits in our family that I either condone or practice myself? Sometimes small changes can have big results. As you read the following ideas, you may see some small changes you could make.

❦

"Do not let any unwholesome talk come out of your mouths, but only what is helpful for building others up according to their needs, that it may benefit those who listen" (Eph. 4:29). Talk about the meaning of this verse as a family.

&.

Teach your children to be empathetic. The Sioux Indians had a prayer, "Great Spirit, help us never to judge another until we have walked for two weeks in his moccasins."

&.

Let your children see you listening with patience. Don't hurry the other person. Show the courtesy of listening to what he or she has to say no matter how much you may disagree.

&.

"There are two sides to every question"—Protagoras. Remember this when you're called upon to referee an argument.

&.

Identify the consistent conflicts in your home—whose turn it is to feed the dog or do the dishes, how many minutes someone gets to play a video game, how much time is spent on the telephone, etc. Meet together as a family and map out simple guidelines of fairness.

&.

"Youth today loves luxury. They have bad manners, contempt for authority, no respect for older people, and talk nonsense when they should work. Young people do not stand up any longer when adults enter the room. They contradict their parents, talk too much in company, guzzle their food, lay their legs on the table, and tyrannize their elders"—Socrates, describing the young people of Athens in 500 B.C. Take comfort in the fact that your children probably don't have worse manners and relational skills than any other children in the history of the world.

🐖

Stop yelling, and talk as a family about how you're all going to stop yelling. "A gentle answer turns away wrath, / but a harsh word stirs up anger" (Prov. 15:1).

🐖

If your child invites an ill-mannered guest over to your home, when the guest leaves, instruct your child in private about appropriate behavior and how to behave as a guest in someone else's home.

🐖

Plan regular individual outings with each of your children. They each need some one-on-one time with you when they don't have to compete with a sibling for your attention.

🐖

"Build for your team a feeling of oneness, of dependence on one another and of strength to be derived by unity"— Vince Lombardi. Teach your kids that a family is a team of people on each other's side and committed to each other's good.

🐖

Create a "Swine-Fine" bucket. I painted a picture of a pig on the top of a white plastic bucket and kept it on my kitchen counter. Whenever one of the boys used poor manners or behaved disrespectfully toward a family member, I called out "swine fine!" He was required to deposit a designated amount of money (which I got to keep) in my bucket.

§

Make a list of the names and negative phrases you would like to eliminate from your family's vocabulary. Sit down together and talk about how each person feels when these things are said to him or her. Agree together to rid them from your conversation.

§

Thank your children for the small things they do, even if it's chores they're supposed to do.

§

"Be kind and compassionate to one another, forgiving each other, just as in Christ God forgave you" (Eph. 4:32). Are there past offenses family members are holding grudges about? Sit down and talk about these honestly.

§

Set aside regular times for family meetings to discern on-going problems and to share successes. Make sure everyone has an opportunity to add to the agenda.

§

"It is not fair to ask of others what you are not willing to do yourself"—Eleanor Roosevelt. Are you modeling the behavior you want your children to embrace?

§

"Finally, all of you, live in harmony with one another; be sympathetic, love as brothers, be compassionate and humble. Do not repay evil with evil or insult with insult, but with blessing, because to this you were called so that you may inherit a blessing" (1 Pet. 3:8–9). Make this a goal of your family.

እ

Make a family rule to never go to bed angry at each other. Settle disputes as soon as possible.

እ

Teach your children to ask before borrowing someone else's belongings. Make sure you do this too.

እ

Treat your children with courtesy. If you're late to pick them up, respond in the same way as if you missed a business appointment. Their time is important too.

እ

Exhibit the kind of manners toward your children's friends as you want them to exhibit toward your friends.

እ

"Good manners is the art of making those people easy with whom we converse. Whoever makes the fewest persons uneasy is the best bred in the company"—Jonathan Swift. No matter what career your children choose, you will do them a favor by teaching them good manners.

እ

Living as a family means learning to put the feelings of others before our own. This means children, as well as Mom and Dad, exhibit self-control even though they feel like slamming a door, throwing something breakable, or hitting someone. Learn to openly and honestly talk out angry feelings. Physical exercise is also a good way to relieve angry feelings.

❧

Never compare your kids to each other or their friends in a derogatory way.

❧

In 1936 Dale Carnegie wrote a book entitled *How to Win Friends and Influence People.* Almost fifty years and fifteen million copies later, businesses all over America continue to use his principles to train employees. I've found these same principles are excellent guidelines for family relationships. When our boys enter high school, I offer a reward for reading this book, knowing it will help them get along not only with siblings, but schoolmates, teachers, and coaches as well. They learn the importance of becoming genuinely interested in other people, smiling, how remembering a person's name shows respect for that person, being a good listener, etc.—habits that will help them throughout life.

❧

Create your own set of family rules. Set a goal for every family member to strive to live by them.

5

Teenagers: A Mother's Guide to Cool

$\mathscr{E}$very mother in the world worries about her children turning into teenagers and staging a family coup. Not to worry. They don't have the stamina to take over. They're too sluggish. Their arteries are clogged with chips and pizza.

For many women, just the thought of a child turning thirteen brings on premature menopause. As for me, I looked forward to our boys becoming teenagers. (I begin therapy next week.) Maybe it's because I failed to master the skills needed in earlier stages of motherhood. I mean, what kind of mother keeps a roll of masking tape on the changing table because she never learned to work the tabs on disposable diapers? Or what sort of mother tells her child the tooth fairy works on a deferred payment plan? And what mother would flush her son's pet snake down the toilet and tell him she donated it to the zoo? Far be it from me to confess to any of the above. (I used only electrical tape, paid tooth fairy IOUs within a week, and have *never* flushed a snake—just a lizard.)

Quite frankly, I've enjoyed the teenage years thoroughly—especially since my lobotomy. Things that once would have driven me to an institution now only give me mild hysteria.

Take, for instance, my boys' bedroom. The EPA just *thinks* it has identified the country's top hazardous-waste sites. *Ha!* I'd drink the water from Boston Harbor before I'd let anything left standing in our teenagers' room touch my lips.

And I'm not alone in my feelings. Cockroaches won't step foot in their room. Too dangerous. Houseflies abort at the door. Actually, our blind Labrador retriever is the only living creature who visits their room without fear. She trips and falls regularly anyway.

To sum it up, our teenagers' idea of a shipshape bedroom is the SS *Poseidon*—after the tidal wave.

Oh, they've tried to convince me their room is a spiritual sanctuary. When you enter there's no other choice but to walk the straight and narrow way—and pray you make it to the other side. They've also tried to make their sloppy habits look better by comparing them to my own housekeeping habits.

"Mom, fess up. We're only following your example," John commented assuredly. "I bet James is the only little kid on the block who uses a toilet brush to play king of the hill. Why shouldn't he? It's not used for anything else."

Hating to admit his perception was correct, I acquiesced under pressure. "You're right, John. As long as I'm asking you to improve, I'll set the pace. I'll try to find that brush tomorrow. Maybe it's buried in James's toy box or in the bottom of his closet."

At this point John thought he'd gained some ground in the battle, but when I opened the closet, I *smelled* victory close at hand. The collection of ripe tennis shoes, dirty t-shirts, and mildewed socks ran the air pollution index off the scale. Holding my breath became mandatory. I'm not saying just how bad the closet smelled, but essence of septic tank is putting it mildly.

Forget the hype about solid air fresheners. The one I attached to the closet door melted in five minutes. And don't waste your money on expensive potpourri aerosols. This kind of battle calls for chemical warfare. I concocted my own high-potency disinfectant spray. I don't know what it did to their clothes, but every time I took a breath, I sanitized my lungs.

Okay, maybe I'm being overly negative about their room. My father taught me to always look for the positive. In this situation, at least I can see their understanding of life science has been enhanced. Louis Pasteur could have used their room as a lab—there's always something growing mold.

Another touchy topic mothers of teenagers must deal with is shopping. Actually, I just don't understand moms who gripe and complain about going shopping with their sons or daughters. They should take a tip from me: Always shop alone. John was fifteen before he realized he didn't have to be of "legal age" to enter a department store. For years I picked out the clothes I liked and brought them home on approval for him to try on.

Joel, on the other hand, wasn't as easy to deceive. Not unlike mothers who feel disappointed when their kindergartners discover there is no Santa Claus, I was crushed when Joel learned that clothing stores actually have dressing rooms. Now he always wants to go shopping with me, and I've discovered two equally important components to a positive parent-teen shopping experience: a gold card with a generous line of credit and a mild sedative. Just shopping for ordinary jeans with a teenager is enough to make a Baptist order a stiff drink.

In my case, I didn't mind spending a little extra money when the boys went through the designer jeans era.

I didn't mind shopping at seventeen different stores for just the right shade of "faded" when they wanted stone-washed jeans.

I didn't even complain when I had to spring for cowboy boots and hat when they were in the roper jeans phase.

But when they asked me to buy brand-new jeans so they could cut holes in the knees, I had to draw the line.

"Why, for the love of peace, do you want to wear 100 percent cotton, favorite-logo boxer shorts, a colorful, interlock-knit shirt, braided-leather belt, color-coordinated socks, expensive shoes, and a watch that does everything but logarithms—with jeans that have holes in the knees?" I asked pointedly.

"Because it's studly," Joel replied matter-of-factly. "Come on, Mom. We've seen old picture albums from when you were a teenager. Don't try telling us holey jeans are worse than hip-hugger jeans. Let's talk about who really looks the stupidest."

Thankfully, the holey-jean look didn't last long. As a matter of fact I was about ready to get into it myself—in an entrepreneurial sort of way. Instead of giving away old winter slacks, I figured I could let moths eat holes in the knees—and get top dollar at my garage sale.

Looking back, I think it was the jeans issue that stimulated me to write my "Memo to Resident Teenagers"—otherwise known as my get-them-to-do-what-you-want-them-to-do-by-telling-them-the-opposite theory. I found this method works well with almost any issue you are tired of arguing about. (Eat your hearts out, Dr. Dobson and Dr. Brazelton. You only wish you'd thought of this brilliant technique first.)

Memo to Resident Teenagers

1. Illegal possession of healthy food will not be tolerated. Anyone caught snacking on fresh fruit and vegetables will be grounded.

2. Dirty clothes hampers will be inspected periodically without prior warning. The persons responsible for receptacles containing clothes that are actually dirty will be prosecuted. *Do not under any circumstance do your own laundry.*

3. Television viewing will be strictly monitored. Less than four hours per day will not be tolerated. Teenagers who sneak time to do their homework, practice a musical instrument, work on a hobby, exercise, or attend any sort of youth group during these hours will face severe consequences.

4. All teenagers are required to spend at least two hours daily on the telephone. These calls must include one of the following: one friend you met at summer camp who lives a minimum of three states away, one girl we don't like, or one 900 number. Failure to comply with this rule may result in bodily harm.

5. As a responsible mother, I will keep close watch over all music. I want to hear only heavy metal and rap music with questionable lyrics— played at no less than thirty-two decibels. Any classical, inspirational, easy-listening instrumental, or quality movie soundtracks will be confiscated and destroyed.

Trust me. This works.

But try as we may, there are still some circumstances mothers of teenagers cannot manipulate. So we might as well face the music—and just hope it's not 2 Live Crew. There's one occasion in particular that strikes fear in the heart of every mother. It's the day she is never closer to a coronary: driver's license day.

You take your average mother. She bites her fingernails to the quick, gains five pounds from nervous snacking, and tries to sedate herself with cough syrup—all to no avail. Her child still passes the driver's test.

Me? I wait with bated breath until I have a driver I can order to run my errands and carpool the other kids. The way I see it, teenage drivers are a heckuvalot safer than a thirty-year-old mother with a three-ring circus in the back of her minivan. Or a forty-year-old man in midlife crisis who fixates on every red sports car that passes by. Or a fifty-plus man—still in midlife crisis—who makes spur-of-the-moment U-turns because the cute, thirtysomething driver is now more interesting than the red car itself.

There's no doubt my teenagers are better drivers than I am. Just ask our insurance agent. I'm one of her few clients who has received a speeding ticket in a zoo parking lot, had a curb jump out in front of me (causing $750 damage), and dented a brand-new Acura while trying to parallel park my Suburban in a space designed for a golf cart.

Actually, my driving record works to my advantage when I'm under a tight writing deadline and need the teenagers to do extra chores around the house. I simply threaten to stop writing and open a driving school. Believe me, your house hasn't been deep cleaned until you've had two teenagers scrubbing everything in sight from fear of starvation.

If your kids happen to be better drivers than you are, or better at any other skill or behavior you prize, don't be adolescent about it yourself. Their being good at something does not take away from you. It is, at any number of levels, a credit to you. Praise them and use their skill. I have my teenage driver run errands, wash the car, and drive me places. When you're running late, it's much easier to put on your makeup in the car if you're not driving.

Driving automobiles is, whether we like it or not, part of modern living. We can worry, resist, fuss, and fume when our kids begin to drive. Or we can go with the traffic flow, taking the opportunity to teach our kids responsibility: He who drives pays for his own gas. Consequences: He who leaves the gas tank empty has to get out of bed at 7:00 A.M. Saturday morning when Mom gets stranded at exercise class. Helping others: He who drives can volunteer to take Grandma to the doctor. The list could go on, but I think you get the idea.

As a matter of fact, going with the traffic flow and taking advantage of opportunities as they arise doesn't just apply to teenagers and driving. It applies to teenagers and life. And it's an attitude opportunity or problem—ours, not theirs—depending on how we look at it. We can rejoice with our teens in their newfound skills, let them practice independence, and point out their mistakes in judgment based on lack of experience. Or we can try to stop them from learning new things, try to make all their decisions for them because they don't have experience, and point to their mistakes as evidence that we think they'll never grow up to be responsible adults. And if we think they won't, chances are, despite the law of contrary, they'll do everything in their power to prove us right.

I would be remiss if I didn't stop here and point out one other anxiety-producing topic of mothers with teenagers: dating.

Mark the day when your pre-teenager first notices the opposite sex as something other than a punching bag, because things will never be the same. At first, their behavioral changes are extreme. Boys begin to bathe without being told and apply multiple layers of deodorant—gluing the skin in their armpits together. Girls show up at breakfast one morning looking like they applied their makeup with a spray gun. Both smell like they fell into a vat of cologne.

Just take it in stride. They settle down (we hope) by their twentieth birthday.

The most important thing to remember during this stage is *never* to embarrass your teenager in front of the opposite sex. If you blow it in this area, it's only a matter of time before you'll be reading tabloid headlines such as: "Teenager Wins Right to Institutionalize Mother in Emotional Abuse Suit." To avoid any behaviors that might embarrass your teenagers, keep the following guidelines handy.

A Mother's Guide to Cool

1. If a teenager asks if your head got caught in a ceiling fan, it's time for a new hair style.

2. If you hear your teenager's friends refer to you using the term "Dork Massive," take the hint and update your wardrobe.

3. Never admit your favorite television program is "The Flying Nun."

4. Never do your Doris Day impersonation in front of teenagers.

5. Never laugh with cottage cheese in your mouth.

6. If your teenager asks if all mothers wear support hose under their bathing suits, don't show up at their next pool party.

7. If you hear a song from your era on the radio, remember teenagers consider mime your best range.

8. Don't brag about the time you won the Miss Bell Aircraft Second Shift beauty contest.

9. Understand that teenagers couldn't care less about what happened when you were their age.

10. Never offer your teenager's friends liver, tuna casserole, or prune juice.

However, there are some instances, embarrassing or not, when a mother must speak up. I think it's perfectly normal to firmly insist your son's date borrow your turtleneck sweater if she shows up wearing a tube top—in December. It's reasonable to question your daughter's boyfriend when he installs a Murphy bed in the back of his pickup truck. And when a guy shows up at your door with ink designs on 80 percent of his body—and he doesn't work in the Mont Blanc quality-control department—it's okay to turn to your daughter and just say no.

Of course the ideal is that our teenagers would recognize potentially risky situations and react responsibly on their own. The problem is—when it comes to the opposite sex—most teenagers do not operate with their clutches fully engaged.

We've found it helps tremendously for kids to not only learn how to make wise decisions from their parents, but also from older peers they look up to. That's one reason we're big believers in sending kids to good youth camps.

We attribute many of the positive characteristics we see in our teenagers to the influence of good counselors at summer camp. It has been our custom to send our kids to camp every summer after their second-grade year. I'll never forget the first year John and Joel went off together for two weeks. I couldn't eat. I paced the floor. I couldn't help but worry—what if they came back early?

The morning I took them to meet the camp bus, I watched my trip to Florida, antique bedroom furniture, and new refrigerator climb aboard. At departure time I found their heads looking out the tinted window.

What I said: "Bye guys! Just be your wonderful selves and have a great time. Dad and I love you and will be thinking about you."

What I thought: "Do you have any idea how much this camp costs? For all we've sacrificed, you'd better have the time of your life and bring home all your dirty clothes!"

After the first summer our kids went to camp, we decided if this was going to be an annual event, the guys would need to earn some of the money to cover the cost. For ten years they've done just that. And it has been worth every penny to them and to us.

At camp they've learned flexibility, independence, and responsibility. They have also enhanced their athletic and social skills, developed self-discipline, and grown in character—at least somewhat. Last summer, after ten years of camp, I was hoping to get a letter from John that confirmed how much he had grown in character.

This is the letter I wanted to get:

Dearest Mother and Father,

My camp experience thus far has been very stimulating. I won the camp tennis tournament, was elected captain of the baseball team, have learned quite a few new skills, have developed meaningful relationships with many new friends, was elected best all-around camper by the counselors, and read the Old Testament in my spare time. It has occurred to me during this tenth year of camp that you have had a significant influence on my life. Thank you for being such wonderful parents and for sacrificing so much of your time and money to help me develop to my full potential.

Your loving son,

John

This is the letter I got:

Hi Mom and Dad,

My cabin's the best ever. Well, that's all the news from camp where all the men are strong, the women are good-looking, and the activities are above average.

Love ya,

John

P.S. Please send:
> more clothes
> more money
> CD player
> new tennis racquet
> Jenny

Overall, I can truthfully say camp is a positive experience for all of us. It's nice for the kids—and the parents—to have a short change of scenery and a rest from each other. And camp counselors can teach our kids things we can't. I don't know about you, but I'm not big on getting up at 5 A.M. to hike thirty miles in the rain, starting a fire with wet matches, and cooking breakfast over said fire. So let the camp counselors teach them whatever lesson is to be learned from an experience like that. Camp provides parents an opportunity to learn too. We can learn to use other resources than our own and other people to help teach our kids life skills we know they'll need. And it's good for our kids to hear someone else besides Mom and Dad—like a cool counselor they admire—reinforce strong values about topics such as dating and sex.

I have to admit that, for the most part, living with teenagers has been a delight. Many days their helpful attitudes and fun-loving personalities bring me great joy in the midst of stress. Please don't think I'm taking the credit for this. And don't think I don't know things can change—even before this book hits the shelves. There are no guarantees—for any parent. But I strongly believe what kind of parent-leader I am has a lot to do with whether our teenagers will want to follow me.

Over the years, Bill and I have read countless books and articles on the subject of leadership. Bill now teaches seminars at corporations and churches on the subject of leadership. At one particular seminar, a group of department heads were discussing the power of informal leadership—how a person without an official leadership title or position can be very influential. They concluded that mothers were perhaps the strongest informal leaders in the world. I believe this is true. Judie Byrd, a good friend and an outstanding mother in my opinion, often comments in her homemaking classes that a woman has more power over what goes on in her family than her husband does as head of a company.

If a mother's leadership is indeed so powerful in the lives of her children, we would do well to strive to be the best mother-leaders we can be. In Bill's seminar, he lists ten characteristics of highly effective leadership. I've adapted these to my role as mother-leader.

1. *Leaders have a strong sense of purpose.* They know where they are going. They stand for something. They are not easily blown off course. They know what they want to achieve and focus their energy on getting there.

In this day of vacillating values, I think it is crucial for mothers to have a strong mooring to a purpose bigger than themselves. Teenagers need to know their family's purpose or vision—and that it is firmly fixed. They need constants that serve as anchors for them in the turbulent sea of adolescence.

In our own family, we've talked about why each of us might be here on planet earth at this particular time in history, and why God might have put us together in the particular family unit that he did. We've encouraged each boy to think about what his overall purpose might be—no matter what career he chooses. And we decided corporately that our family purpose would be to create an atmosphere in our home where each family member might be nurtured and encouraged to become all God wants him or her to be so that we might make an impact on our culture—individually and corporately—in a positive way. Our decisions revolve around this purpose.

2. *Leaders are persistent.* They are willing to put in the time and effort required to reach their goal. Persistence separates the leader from the dreamer.

Let's face it. Motherhood is hard work. It demands patience, sacrifice, tenacity, long hours at low pay, and resilience under fire. This is not a ladylike image. But sometimes we have to be bulldog stubborn. Winston Churchill reminded us, "The nose of a bulldog has been slanted backward so that it can breathe without letting go."

There are times we have to take a strong stand against blatantly immoral movies and television shows *everyone else's* mom allows. Sometimes we must turn off the radio and talk about the questionable lyrics of a song *everyone else* thinks is okay. And sometimes our stubborn commitment is displayed in our refusal to give up on a child. This kind of care and tenacity sounds loud and clear in the ears of their minds. No one else's music can drown it out. God challenges us to "run with endurance the race that is set before us, fixing our eyes on Jesus, the author and perfecter of faith, who for the joy set before Him endured the cross, despising the shame" (Heb. 12:1–2 NASB). Sometimes the race is long and hard, but we don't have to run it alone.

3. Leaders take risks. Leaders take calculated gambles with people, money, and ideas. The prospects of not trying are more onerous than not succeeding.

As mothers, we take risks every day. I let my son drive a car to school every day during morning rush-hour traffic. Every time he's out on a date, I take a risk. Far too many mothers are overprotective. Children need to have a chance to fail and to make up their own minds. They need to encounter the real world while they are still at home so in case they fall we can help them pick up the pieces. I know many parents who sheltered their children, then released them at eighteen to go off to college. With all their newfound freedom, most crashed and burned. That's not risk. That's stupidity. Children need to experience freedom gradually while we are close by to help. Every time we let out the rope, we take a risk. They could fall. They could abuse their new freedom. But we are close enough to monitor their progress and catch them before they fall too hard.

4. *Leaders are able to attract and energize people.* They are like magnets. They ignite, inspire, and draw people around a common effort or goal. What draws people to a leader? An attitude of servanthood. People want to follow someone who they know has their best interests at heart. That's why people were so attracted to Jesus. He said, "For even the Son of Man did not come to be served, but to serve, and to give his life as a ransom for many" (Mark 10:45).

It might sound redundant to call upon mothers to adopt an attitude of servanthood. It's almost part of the definition of motherhood. But unfortunately, I know women who think of their children as a bother or an imposition they can't wait to get rid of. These women produce double misery. After all, what teenager would want to follow a leader who can't wait until he's gone?

Lamentably, I also meet women who are so insecure they are living their lives through their children. On the surface they look like adoring mothers, but come the teen years when children begin to assert their independence, the truth becomes clear. The mothers are using their children to build their own self-esteem. Kids know this instinctively and find another leader they think they can trust.

5. *Leaders trust their followers.* They are able to establish relationships based on trust, respect, and care. They accept people as they are, don't dwell on past mistakes, and radiate confidence in their followers.

Anyone who accepts the position of motherhood had best be ready to dish out forgiveness or else live in the garbage heap of her own hurt emotions. Teenagers need to be confronted with their irresponsible behavior, but they need heavy doses of forgiveness and unconditional love when they fail. They need to know we trust and have confidence in them even when they don't please us— and even when it's hard to trust them. Henry L. Stimson said, "The chief lesson I have learned in a long life is that the only way to make a man trustworthy is to trust him: and the surest way to make him untrustworthy is to distrust him and show your mistrust." Have you ever thought about the tremendous trust God has in us? He has given us unconditional acceptance, entrusted us with incredible resources of power and ability, and commissioned us to accomplish his cause here on earth. He has a lot more confidence in us than we have in ourselves. Yet none deserve it less.

6. Leaders know their strengths and limitations. They don't try to do everything. They know what they do well and stick to it.

As a mother, I wear a lot of hats—some of which don't fit very well. But a few do fit well, and these are the things I focus on. This is God's will for my life according to 1 Peter 4:10 (NASB), "As each one has received a special gift, employ it in serving one another, as good stewards of the manifold grace of God."

It's no secret my meals should always be served with a side dish of antacids. And when I do laundry, the boys never know if their white underwear will turn out peony pink or baby blue. Because of my domestic flops, I spent many years feeling like I was an inferior mother. Then I decided even if the women who marry my boys want to sue me for neglecting to teach them household skills, at least I could focus on some things I do well in the business arena and enhance their development there.

The guys may not be able to cook, clean, or sew very well, but their business résumés will be pretty stout. Our teenagers have been involved in some type of entrepreneurial venture since the ages of five and nine. They started their own caladium bulb business (with our help) ten years ago and have earned a large percentage of their camp tuition each year. Joel, now age fifteen, is gifted at sales and works part time at a store. At age eighteen, John started his own graphic art and typesetting business. With the profit he made from that business, he started a t-shirt business—creating his own designs. Through their business experience they've learned how to relate to adults, to follow through with responsibilities, treat customers with courtesy, and understand basic economics. (I hope they'll marry women who won't care if their husbands are domestic morons.)

7. *Leaders are learners.* They consider themselves students, not professors. They are humble and can learn from anyone with something to teach them.

It is important for our teenagers that we set the model of teachability. If we come across as having arrived, not only do we miss the opportunity to learn ourselves, but we set an example our teens will follow when we want to teach them something.

One of the greatest and most influential teachers of the twentieth century is Dr. Howard Hendricks. In his book *Teaching to Change Lives* (Multnomah Press, 1987), he tells the story of passing the window of one of his college professors every morning at 5:30 A.M. on his way to work, then again at 11:00 P.M. on his way back home. The professor was always sitting at this window, studying. Finally Dr. Hendricks asked the professor why he kept studying. After all, he was the teacher now. He should already know everything. The professor answered, "Son, I would rather have my students drink from a running stream than a stagnant pool."

This story made a great impression on me as a mother. It impelled me to never stop learning—that I might set an example for my children, be able to understand what my children were studying, and to stimulate their learning process at home.

The day we put our brains on the shelf and stop learning about motherhood—and other subjects as well—is the day we stifle significant communication with our teenagers. Perhaps the philosophy we should strive to live by and to pass on to our kids should be: As long as we live, we learn, and as long as we learn, we live.

8. Leaders love their work. They have a zest, an enthusiasm, about what they do that is contagious.

Motherhood is the greatest job I have been given. It is an incredible privilege I can't believe God has entrusted me with. Of course there are things I don't like about it. There are plenty of days I want to change my name. And there are times I want to scream if I have to wash one more load of clothes, make one more peanut-butter sandwich, and sit through one more school program. But after nineteen years of experience, I can't think of anything I would like to do better. I can't wait until I have grandchildren so I can practice what I learned on the first three.

9. Leaders have a positive attitude. They believe that failures and difficulties are only cleverly disguised opportunities to learn from. Henry Ford said, "Failure is only the opportunity to begin again more intelligently."

If failure were final, my life would have been over years ago. Fortunately, I live with a very gracious, loving, and forgiving husband. And I live for a gracious God, whose attitude is settled toward me in a constant flow of love and acceptance. I figure I owe the same positive outlook to my children. I owe it to them when I fail to get up and learn from my mistake. I owe it to them to treat their failures the same way God treats mine. It's a debt I owe as much to God as to my children. Yet God doesn't need the benefit of my forgiveness. My children do.

10. Leaders are self-disciplined. They don't indulge their fears or their appetites. They take care of the inner part of their lives. The result is integrity. What they say and do is what they are.

Discipline is a part of my life. Years ago I decided there were certain things I would give up in exchange for my health—and the example I set for my children. I decided to give up some unhealthy habits that affected not only my body, but my mind and my spirit. I not only limited my intake of negative things, I replaced them with positive. Every mother has to make the same choices to limit herself in order to achieve a larger goal. I can be like a swamp or a river. A swamp has no boundaries, no limitations—and no impact. A river, on the other hand, is restricted to a channel—and flows with force. No leader or mother can make a positive impact without self-limitations.

What this means in my role as a mother is this: If I ask my children to take care of their bodies, to censor what goes into their minds, to nourish their spirits, and to strive for excellence in their schoolwork, I'd best do the same. I must model the behaviors I want them to embrace.

On the surface, mothers seem to be very different. Some are tall; some are short. Some are pear-shaped; some are apple-shaped. Some are extroverts; some are introverts. Some are polished and sophisticated; some are rough and unrefined. But beneath the surface, differences are common characteristics that distinguish mothers who feel good about the job they're doing and mothers who feel like failures and want to start over.

If you're a mother of teenagers and your relationship is getting worse by the day, maybe you blame yourself and say, "If only I had done this. If only I had done that . . . ," I'd like to suggest you focus your energies in a more positive way. Instead of saying "If only," try saying "What now?" It's never too late to sit down with a child and ask forgiveness for your part in a relational problem—even if you think you're only 5 percent of the problem. Admit your mistakes, confirm your love, and confess you want to want to be a good mother. Ask your teenager to honestly tell you how you can be a better mother. Your willingness to listen and learn will go a long way.

Mothers who feel like their relationship with their teenager is going well know that life is a constantly changing opportunity to learn. As the tide of the relationship ebbs and flows, they ask "What now?" on a regular basis—so as not to be left high and dry and not able to make a meaningful connection with their child.

Family Matters

It's been said that teenagers are children in adult bodies. Another way of putting it is that they're adults one minute and small children the next. And in many ways they don't have the experience and wisdom to make their own decisions or to face life's problems alone. They still need discipline and love. And, most of all, they need to be encouraged, under your courageous mother-leadership, to begin to think and behave responsibly on an adult level. Let these ideas spur your thinking on your role as a leader.

ૄ

Create a warm and welcoming atmosphere in your home so your teenager and his friends will want to hang out there. They'll have a safe, fun place to go, and you'll know what they're doing. Keep plenty of soda and snacks on hand, and be willing to put up with some mess and some louder-than-pleasant music.

ૄ

Take a look at yourself from your teenagers' perspective. Do they look up to you as the type of adult they want to be some day?

ૄ

Create opportunities for your teenagers to be around kids a few years older who can serve as role models. Adopt a college student attending school in your area. Invite him or her over for weekend meals and to share family holidays.

ૄ

Where are you leading your family? Carve an evening out of your schedule and discuss your family's vision and purpose. Vision is a clear mental image of a desired future state. Discuss your teenagers' strengths and abilities, and help them dream grand dreams about what they can achieve. Have each family member write a personal vision statement, then corporately write a vision statement for your family. Think big! Recognize that a vision for the future based only on your present capabilities will be flawed and limited. Remember God can do big things through you and your family. "Now to him who is able to do immeasurably more than all we ask or imagine, according to his power that is at work within us" (Eph. 3:20).

Don't bury your head in the sand. Listen to your children's music. Question the lyrics. I exercise at a class that plays popular music, not only for the exercise, but to keep up with what my kids are hearing on the radio. Ask your kids if they understand what they are putting into their minds. Research shows that when our minds receive an image six times, it becomes indelibly etched there.

"Trust in the LORD with all your heart, / and lean not on your own understanding; / in all your ways acknowledge him, / and he will make your paths straight" (Prov. 3:5–6). When it's time to let your teens stretch their wings and experience a new freedom, remember this verse.

Read *Ten Mistakes Parents Make with Teenagers (and How to Avoid Them)* by Dr. Jay Kesler (Word Publishing, 1988)— preferably *before* you have teenagers.

Help your kids network with other kids who have like values and ambitions. Before Joel started high school we hosted a party for kids he knew from various middle schools who would soon be attending the same high school. Now we try to regularly host simple get-togethers for these kids since they've all become friends.

🙣

"Yield to a man's tastes, and he will yield to your interests"—Edward Bulwar-Lytton. Think about these words. How do you respond to your kids' likes and dislikes?

🙣

What have you learned lately? Are your children drinking from a running stream or a stagnant pool?

🙣

Be aware of teenagers' need to feel good about themselves. Teach them the importance of good hygiene and keep makeup and grooming tools on hand. Let a professional cosmetologist show your daughter how to lightly apply makeup to bring out her natural beauty. Girls and guys may need a regular appointment for a facial to get their pores cleaned out.

🙣

"Being confident of this, that he who began a good work in you will carry it on to completion until the day of Christ Jesus" (Phil. 1:6). Don't give up praying for your teenager even when you don't see any progress.

🙣

"Nothing in the world can take the place of persistence. Talent will not: nothing is more common than unsuccessful men with talent. Genius will not: unrewarded genius is almost a proverb. Education will not: the world is full of educated derelicts. Persistence and determination alone are omnipotent"— Calvin Coolidge. Be persistent in loving your teenager.

૨

Let your teenagers know you're on their team. Show an interest in their friends, schoolwork, and activities without being pushy or judgmental.

૨

Buy a vintage magazine from a flea market. Laugh together about the fashions of your youth.

૨

Don't be afraid to say "I'm sorry." No mother's perfect. Be willing to confirm what your teen already knows.

૨

Do your kids know you like them, or do they think you can't wait until they're out of the nest?

૨

Take your teen and a friend on a special trip. Joel has great memories of when he and his best friend went on a business trip with me.

૨

Think of creative ways to show your teenager your love. One friend becomes the "finals fairy" to relieve the pressure when her daughter is studying for final exams. She buys her small gifts and writes humorous poems.

૨

Take pictures of your children and their friends at special events or just on an ordinary day when they're at your house. Have prints made and let your children send them to their friends.

ॐ

Stand up for right and wrong. Set limits on what they can watch on television as long as they live in your home. Just because they may be able to walk into an R-rated movie doesn't mean you have to condone immoral or violent behavior in your family room.

ॐ

Be vigilant about your teenagers' friends. If they ask to spend time with someone whose values and habits are questionable, let them have the friend over to your house. If you see that the relationship would not be a healthy one for your child and that your child may not be strong enough to be the leader, talk about this openly. When one of our boys wanted to pursue a friendship and hang out socially with a boy we knew was headed for trouble, we had a great opportunity to talk about the importance of choosing good friends and the effect they have on our lives. During this time, Bill and I planned plenty of teenager-friendly activities and weekend family trips so when we said no to some things, we were saying yes to other fun things.

ॐ

Think of ways to show your children you care about their world. Clip magazine and newspaper articles pertaining to subjects they are studying in school. File them by category for easy retrieval when needed.

ॐ

Show your teens you care by treating their schoolwork and desk as you would your own business. Make sure they have plenty of supplies, good lighting, and a pleasant atmosphere in their "offices."

&

Put together a photo album for your child with pictures of him over the years. Present it to him or her at graduation.

&

Help your teenagers give a graduation or going-away party for a friend. This says you care about what's important to them.

&

Buy your daughter a book on a subject she loves or a CD or tape of her favorite artist. Present it to her out of the blue with a note saying "Thanks for being such a terrific gal."

&

Help your teenager start a business or get a job. Brainstorm his or her talents and resources, then think of a need that he or she could meet. Help him or her write a good résumé. Teach him or her the importance of looking people in the eye and shaking hands firmly when being interviewed.

&

"Let us not become weary in doing good, for at the proper time we will reap a harvest if we do not give up" (Gal. 6:9). Ask God to help you hang in there when you feel like giving up.

&

When your children enter the teen years, make a big deal about it. We took our guys to dinner at a nice restaurant and presented each of them with a handsome ring with a cross emblem. We told them the ring could serve as a reminder during their teen years that no matter where they were, God was with them. Then we had a special prayer for them.

🖋

Read *Drug-proof Your Kids* by Steve Arterburn and Jim Burns (Focus on the Family Publishing, 1989).

6

---

*Teaching Values to Kids
and Other Lost Episodes of
"Mission Impossible"*

 here are two occupations that will always receive more
than their fair share of criticism: the president of the
United States and the pastor of a church. People who have
the nerve to accept either of these positions understand
there is no way they can please all of the people even a
small percentage of the time.

Overall, I think our boys have good memories of the
sixteen years Bill served in various capacities at different
churches. As our family interacted with members, the kids
learned a lot about life and people. We made lifelong
friends—and a couple of enemies. We celebrated and cried
with our congregations. We rejoiced in each other's victories and comforted each other in defeat. We prayed, sang,
worshiped, and learned together. Our children grew up
comfortably attending the sacred ceremonies of the
church—communions, baptisms, ordinations, weddings,
funerals—and potluck dinners.

It's not that we didn't want to be open and honest
with our kids about occupational struggles and relationship problems at church. We just decided not to go into
juicy church-fight details and spill our guts after a knock-
down, drag-out board meeting. Besides, how much good

would it really do to tell an eight-year-old that the chairman of the board is a scumball jerk to the tenth degree?

But I wouldn't trade our negative and many times difficult church experiences for anything. Painfully, looking back with twenty-twenty hindsight, I now see conflicts are never one-sided. Bill and I played our part in the conflicts as well. But through these less-than-ideal situations we learned a very important truth, and it's a truth we want to pass on to our children: Nobody's perfect—we're all jerks saved by grace. It's an amazing thing to ponder—that in spite of our weaknesses, frailties, bad attitudes, and sinful behavior—God graciously forgives us, loves us unconditionally, and continues to use us to fulfill his purposes. We want our children to know and to love this God who loves us with such an extravagant love, and we want them to embrace the values he sets forth in his Word.

Nor, because they spent the early years of their lives as preacher's kids, would I want our children to base their opinion of God on the behavior and attitudes of some of his children in the church. We wanted the boys to form their opinion of God and his truth as objectively as possible from the Bible and from what they picked up from us at home, as well as on what they saw at church, because what they saw at church often had very little to do with knowing a loving God.

Take potluck dinners. It is my opinion that next to National Shampoo Week and Dictionary Day, potluck dinners are among the most overrated events in the world. Why churches think they can't have a meeting without a potluck dinner is beyond me. Every time Bill wrote the words "potluck dinner" on our calendar, I broke out in hives. I knew I'd labor for two hours in the kitchen, which—besides a public restroom out of toilet paper—is my least favorite place to be, only to have church member after church member stare at my culinary masterpiece, then pass it up.

I tried paying my kids to take large helpings of my recipes as they passed through the potluck line, but they turned me down flat. The money wasn't worth the risk. Actually, the only time my dish disappeared quickly was the time I fixed meatloaf and the church was in the middle of a building program. Someone used it as a brick.

The way I see it, if God had meant for churches to have potluck dinners, Solomon would have built a fellowship hall. Frankly, if I never attend another one, I will die a happy woman.

But try as we may, even if we are clergy families, we can't force our faith upon our children. Sure, we can take them to church every time the door is open, sign them up for every church camp and mission trip, and reward them when they memorize Scripture verses and read the Bible every day. But there's no guarantee that when they grow up our kids will believe what we want them to believe, make the choices we want them to make, and do the things we want them to do.

Although we can't pressure our kids into accepting our values and beliefs any more than we can force them to choose food I've cooked at a potluck dinner, we can influence their decisions by what we teach them in our homes. Children who grow up thinking God is harsh, demanding, and unforgiving—the great Cop in the sky who's out to *get* those he catches in disobedience—have a tendency to do what is right only if they think someone is watching. Kids who grow up learning God is some kind of distant cosmic Santa Claus to whom they can pray when they need something have a propensity to think of the principles he sets forth in his Word as optional and sometimes an imposition to daily living. But kids who grow up learning that

God is not only a holy God, but a forgiving and loving God who cares about every detail of their lives will be more likely to want to know this God. They will also be more likely to want to obey him and please him—even when Mom and Dad aren't around.

I never cease to be amazed when I read the first chapter of the book of Daniel. Here is a young man in his early teens—kidnapped from his homeland and snatched from his family. It puzzles me how he could survive—much less flourish spiritually—in an atmosphere permeated with idolatry and perversion. He endured the influence of an education and a culture that contradicted almost everything a young Jewish boy had been taught.

I've often wondered what it was that kept Daniel from succumbing to peer pressure. How did he resist the temptation to believe his God had abandoned him? And what motivated him to live a life of integrity and obedience before God—and as a result change the culture where he lived? Since home is the place where life makes up its mind, I think it's safe to assume Daniel's parents are a big part of the answer.

For several generations before Daniel, the baton of God's truth had been fumbled badly. Spiritually speaking, things were bad. So bad in fact, the Jews had actually lost the Holy Scriptures. When King Josiah was repairing the temple, he found them under the rubble. As the king read the Holy Scriptures—for the first time in years—he tore his clothes as an act of deep remorse over the sin that filled the land. In the spiritual awakening that followed, many people returned to the worship of the one true God. (See 2 Kings 22–23.) It is very likely that Daniel's parents were converts of this revival, and this made a difference in their family. They picked up the baton of spiritual truth and passed it on to their son. This is the way God intended the relay of spiritual truth to happen.

> The primary place for the flag of truth to be handed on is in the family. The truth was meant to be given from generation to generation. If those who knew God and who had so very much to tell about Him had always been faithful, and had always stuck to the commands or rules of the relay, there would have been no gaps. Each generation would have learned from the one before. Fathers and mothers were to tell sons and daughters. . . .
>
> God's direct Word comes to us—consider your place in the family as central, not just in this moment of history, but as part of the "relay." Don't let a gap come because of you. Don't take the beauty of the family life—and the reality of being able to hand down true truth to one more generation—as a light thing. It is one of the central commands of God. . . . not a responsibility to be handed over to the church and Sunday school.[1]

I believe Daniel's parents understood and fulfilled their responsibility to pass on spiritual truth to their son. They taught him well and prepared him to stand on his own. But they probably never imagined what their teaching would ultimately mean and the extent to which his values would be tested.

I don't know what teaching methods Daniel's parents used, but Bill and I discovered when the kids were small that no one in our family had the time—nor the attention span—for long, boring Bible studies. But we wanted to instill the principles of the Bible in our children. We also wanted them to grow up knowing that God is not only the

Creator of the universe, but the Author of fun. To do this, we decided to strive to live out the values we wanted our three boys to embrace and to follow this advice in Deuteronomy 6:4–7, which urges us to seize teachable moments in the course of everyday life to teach our children Judeo-Christian ethics:

> O Israel, listen: Jehovah is our God, Jehovah alone. You must love him with all your heart, soul, and might. And you must think constantly about these commandments I am giving you today. You must teach them to your children and talk about them when you are at home or out for a walk, at bedtime and the first thing in the morning. (TLB)

Children need more than indoctrination—isolated, formal teaching of spiritual truth. They need initiation—immersing them in a spiritual value system that lets them see, experience, and hear spiritual truth in the midst of everyday living. The power of the truth is not contained in words, but words coupled with deeds. Kids need more than to hear the truth. They need to see truth incarnated in their parents' lives—in the daily routines of life. Like seeing Mom and Dad spend time daily communing with God through Bible study and prayer. Like hearing Mom and Dad treat each other with respect even when they get mad or differ in opinion. Like watching Dad turn off a television program because it glamorizes sin.

Although we don't know what challenges our own children will face, what decisions they'll be forced to make, or what choices will come their way, one thing's for sure. The spiritual lessons—good or bad—they learn in the family, will make a big difference in what values they embrace and whether or not they will live by these values. Dr. Armand Nicholi of Harvard Medical School concurs:

Our family experience is the most significant experience of our lives. Regardless of differences in cultural, social, educational and religious backgrounds, we all share the experience of being a child and for good or evil, spending our days of childhood in the context of the family. Here the seed is sown for what we become as adults. Early family experience determines our adult character structure, the inner picture we harbor of ourselves, how we feel about ourselves, how we perceive and feel about others, our concept of right and wrong—that is, the fundamental rules of human conduct that we call morality.[2]

It's a tragedy when parents don't understand the impact they have on the lives of their children—for good or evil. Maybe they don't understand the importance of teaching children about God and his values. Or perhaps even worse, they forsake their role as teachers and purposefully leave their children on their own to form their opinions and decide what's right and wrong—without guidance.

William Coleridge once talked with a man who did not believe in giving children spiritual guidance. His theory was that the child's mind should not be prejudiced in any direction, so that he could choose his opinions for himself. The great poet said nothing in response, but asked if his visitor would like to see his garden. The man said he would and Coleridge took him to the garden, where only weeds were growing. The man looked at Coleridge in surprise and said, "Why, this is not a garden! There is nothing but weeds here!"

"Well you see," answered Coleridge, "I didn't want to infringe upon the liberty of the garden in any way. I was giving the garden a chance to express itself and choose its own production."

In the book of Proverbs, Solomon gets to the heart of the matter about teaching children values. In Proverbs 23:7 he wrote, "As he thinketh in his heart, so is he" (KJV). This verse reminds me that communicating values and teaching spiritual truths to my children is more than pouring Bible verses into their heads. It is penetrating their *hearts* with spiritual truth. Whether I am successful at this transplant has very little to do with where I go to church, which version of the Bible I read, or how many Vacation Bible Schools I send my kids to. Instead, it rests heavily on how well I teach and communicate the truths I want my children to embrace.

Socrates summarized three components of effective teaching and communication in what he called *ethos* (character), *pathos* (compassion), and *logos* (content). As a mother who wants to pass on spiritual truth to my children, to me this means:

1.   *Who I am is more important than what I say.* My greatest leverage in teaching my children is my *ethos*, or character. What I teach them (and they're learning something from me—whether I like it or not) must be more than merely passing on facts and information. It must be an overflow of my life. When my kids see continuity in what I'm teaching and how I'm living, this gives them confidence and trust in me as a teacher.

I like to take John or Joel with me to speaking engagements or to do radio programs whenever possible. This provides good, one-on-one time while we're traveling, and we enjoy meeting interesting people. But more importantly, it's a good check system for me. Whatever I exhort other mothers to do, I'd best be doing myself—or get called on the carpet by one of my children for not practicing what I'm preaching.

2. *My children must know how much I care before they'll care how much I know.* *Pathos*, or compassion, has to do with our emotions and feelings. As a mother, I must try to understand and care about the emotional makeup of my children—as well as their intellectual and spiritual being. All are equally important. When my children sense that I love them, try to understand their feelings, and have compassion toward them, this produces motivation to learn what I want them to learn and to do what I want them to do. On the other hand, they will not accept my values if they don't value their relationship with me.

If one of the boys is put down by a girl, I need to understand and be sensitive to his hurt. This might mean dropping my work to plan a special spur-of-the-moment family outing to get his mind off the pain. Or if a boy doesn't make a sports team he tried out for, that might mean thinking of some special ways to encourage him and helping him find another outlet for his skills and energy.

3. *I must provide evidence that the message I am teaching is relevant to daily living.* It's important that I communicate the *logos*—or content of the truth—in practical ways so my kids can see the logic and reason behind it. The truth I want them to learn must be woven into the fabric of everyday family life.

If I want my children to understand that the Ten Commandments are not just suggestions, then I must strive to obey them myself. So, knowing the eighth commandment reads "You shall not steal," when I return something at a department store, if the clerk makes an error and gives me back more money than I paid for the item, I point out the error and give back the extra money.

But even if I'm an excellent teacher—exhibiting character, compassion, and content—unless I communicate my message from a position of humility, there's a good chance my children will not value my "pearls of wisdom." Just because I'm the adult doesn't mean I'm always right. I am a learner, just like my children. Sure, I want to stay one step ahead of them, but I try never to forget that I myself am still en route and have a long way to go.

A mother who feels she has to be right all the time will cause real problems between her and her children. I'm not fooling anyone but myself when I try to come across as an expert or a person who has arrived. I could get away with this kind of attitude—or so it seemed—when the kids were younger. But not with teenagers. They can smell a phony a mile away.

If I admit I am not always right, the obvious corollary is that I can be wrong. In my case, I am often wrong. I try to remember the importance of communicating my imperfection to my children. A forty-five-year-old friend shared with me how he has never respected his mother. To this day he does not enjoy a close relationship with her because she has never been willing to say "I was wrong." How sad.

In my own family and in observing hundreds of others, I've witnessed a lot of screwups. It has been reassuring to see that children are amazingly resilient to parental mistakes—if the parents are willing to admit the mistakes and sincerely say "I'm sorry." But the rigid inability to say, "I was wrong—could you forgive me?" does irreparable damage between parent and child.

It goes against my perfectionistic grain to admit failure. But this is a character flaw within myself I'm committed to working on. It helps when I remember that failing to admit my mistakes as a mother to my children can seriously compromise my impact. But confessing my faults to my children can bring amazing healing and bonding. Bill still remembers an incident that happened when he was fifteen. His father walked into his bedroom with tears streaming down his cheeks. He asked Bill's forgiveness for putting so much pressure on him about making good grades. This act of humility increased Bill's love and respect for his dad, and the freedom from pressure caused Bill to make better grades. To this day Bill's eyes get moist when he tells this story.

This happening from Bill's past is indelibly etched on my mind. It reminds me that I'm not only a mother and teacher, I'm a student myself—still on a steep learning curve.

I have to confess, it's one thing to write a book and record all the spiritual truth my mind can spill out. It's easy to get away with the old philosophy, "Do as I say . . ." because most of you will never see what I do. But with my kids, I have to live this stuff on a daily basis. They could care less that their mother gets mail every day from readers telling her what a spiritual blessing she is to them. The way I become a spiritual blessing to my children is to show them the reality of God in my life every day.

If I want them to learn to obey God's principles for living, I must obey. If I want them to take God seriously in their relationships, I must take God seriously in my relationships. If I want them to learn honesty, my children must observe my integrity. If I want them to love and respect others, they must see how I love and respect others—starting with the members of my family. The apostle Luke recorded these pointed words of Jesus Christ: "A student is not above his teacher, but everyone who is fully trained will be like his teacher" (Luke 6:40). As a mother, I see this as the bottom line of teaching my children spiritual truth.

When I was a young mother, I spent a lot of time thinking about what I wanted to teach my children and what I wanted them to be like when they grew up. The older I get, the more I think about the kind of person *I* need to be so that when my kids grow up and are like me, I will like what they have become.

In case you haven't noticed, teaching spiritual values to children is a very difficult swim—upstream. Not only is it hard to consistently practice what we preach, but if we're teaching God's principles—hoping our children will live lives of integrity and strong values—we're going against the grain of culture. Every night when the television goes on, our children see dishonesty, immorality, violence, murder, and a blatant disrespect for any kind of authority—not characteristics we want to see manifested in their lives. But what they see and hear cannot help but affect the lifestyle they choose and the decisions they make. A commitment to instill God's principles and values in our children is an important and worthy battle—a battle for their very lives.

Family Matters

We all need to be reminded every once in a while of the critical importance of teaching our children God's values. We don't do this by organizing some kind of big-deal family Bible hour where Mom or Dad reads from the book of Leviticus while the children fidget and fret, but by weaving God's truths into the fabric of everyday life. Maybe something from this list of things that have worked for us will give you some fresh ideas.

᠄᠊

Learning spiritual truth can make our children wise in many areas of life. But in order to teach our children spiritual truths, we have to spend time together. Philosophy professor Allan Bloom in *The Closing of the American Mind* notes that in the past the family was the true seat of religious training and that the impulse to educate flowed from it. He believes one of the reasons today's students come to the university with no sense of "the great revelations, epics, and philosophies" is "the dreariness of the family's landscape. . . ." Spend time talking with your children and learning together.

Be aware you're in a battle with irresponsible media for teaching values to your kids. Movies and especially television tend to portray Judeo-Christian ethics and family values as subjects of ridicule and contempt. Discuss and learn from what you watch by asking questions such as: What was the message of this program? What were the values of the characters? What would you do to help any of the characters? Was there anything in the program you did not agree with? Did this show portray life as it really is? What in the program uplifted you or motivated you to be a better person? Was it worth your time to watch it?

If we want our children to take a stand on what's right and what's wrong, we must do so ourselves.

Remember this: What we leave *in* our children is far more important than what we leave *to* them.

Understand that kids won't buy a double standard. A mother who wants her children to adopt the principle that sex outside of marriage is wrong may send a double message if the family schedule revolves around her favorite nighttime soap opera because she can't wait to watch and see who goes to bed with whom.

&

What spiritual values are you passing down to your children? Bill remembers that his dad prayed for fifty people every day. Today prayer is an extremely important and regular part of Bill's life—and he has even written a book about it, *What God Does When Men Pray* (NavPress, 1993).

&

Help your children get involved in a church youth group or Bible study. Peers with like values can help each other live up to high standards.

&

Read *Our Journey Home: What Parents Are Doing to Preserve Family Values* by Gary Bauer (Word Publishing, 1992).

&

Walk out of movies that offend your values. Most theaters will either give you your money back or a pass for another movie if you walk out up to halfway through the show.

&

Teach your children that character is always lost when a personal standard is sacrificed on the altar of conformity and popularity.

&

Talk about God during the course of everyday living. Watch the evening news and discuss how sad he must be when his creatures rebel against his laws. Remind your children he is with them when they get out of the car to go to school. Thank him spontaneously for blessings such as your family dog, a home with running water, medicine and doctors, and plenty of food to eat.

❧

"Neutral men are the devil's allies"—E. Chapin. If your kids don't stand for something, they may fall for anything. Talk about what you stand for as family.

❧

Pray with your children before bed every night.

❧

Pray at the breakfast table each morning that each family member would remember God's presence that day.

❧

"All I have seen," wrote Emerson, "teaches me to trust the Creator for all I have not seen." Teach your children to notice and enjoy God in the beauty of his creation.

❧

"I have hidden your word in my heart / that I might not sin against you" (Ps. 119:11). Set up a fun and creative reward system to help your child memorize Scripture.

❧

Is God's word important and relevant in your own life? If so, live your life so that your children know it is.

❧

Our children must understand that God didn't give us the Ten Commandments to frustrate us. He did not look down and say, "Hmmm, how can I make those creatures miserable? If they enjoy something, I think I'll make a law against it!" The laws of God are not illogical ordinances written by some power-hungry, sadistic god. They are sensible rules given by a wise and loving God for the greatest good of his people.

🖐

Read a passage of Scripture aloud at the breakfast table from a modern translation of the Bible. Get into the habit of starting your day by acknowledging your Creator and his Word.

🖐

See to it that your own spiritual life is growing so you will have something to offer your children. Water it regularly with prayer, Bible study, and fellowship with spiritually minded people.

🖐

"First I make my decisions, then my decisions make me"—Howard Hendricks. Teach your children that the decisions we make daily form us into what we will be to-morrow. Small decisions can have a big result—for good or for bad.

🖐

Set aside some time to make a list of the values you want to pass on to your children. Think about the best way to get these across.

🖐

Buy your children their own modern translation of the Bible. Our teenagers like the *Youth Walk Devotional Bible*

(Zondervan, 1992). Second grader James enjoys the *International Children's Bible* (Word Publishing, 1988).

એ

"Try not to become a man of success but rather try to become a man of value"—Albert Einstein. Our culture tells our children that success is all-important. We need to tell them otherwise.

એ

Encourage and reward your children for reading good books with strong values.

એ

Write and ask to be put on the Focus on the Family mailing list. This organization has excellent resources for parents and children of all ages. (Focus on the Family, Colorado Springs, Colorado 80995)

એ

"How can a young man keep his way pure? / By living according to your word" (Ps. 119:9). I know of no better way to help my children keep their way pure than by instilling God's Word in their minds and hearts.

એ

Read aloud as a family good books that teach sound values. Learn together from the lives of the characters.

એ

Be straightforward and trusting when asking about questionable situations. For example, if you find a note in your child's room that refers to a friend's drinking, instead of trying to set a trap like, "Do you or your friends drink?

No? Then explain this note!" say something like, "I found this note in your room that concerns me. Could we talk about it?" If you come across in a punitive, authoritarian, or mistrusting way, you'll have a defensive child who learns to lie, conceal, and mistrust you.

❦

"All Scripture is God-breathed and is useful for teaching, rebuking, correcting and training in righteousness, so that the man of God may be thoroughly equipped for every good work" (2 Tim. 3:16–17). Teach your kids to respect the Bible as God's Word to his children and relevant to every issue in life.

❦

Make sure your children understand that loving God does not mean turning off the mind. Create an atmosphere where they can openly ask questions and work through their beliefs. Honest questions, and even honest doubts, deserve honest discussion and honest answers.

7

Visit to a Dud Ranch: Tips on Making Fun Family Memories

*W*hy is it every time I call "Dinner's ready!" my family scatters? Bill heads for the bathroom with the last three issues of *National Geographic*. John informs me he's developed an interest in nutrition—and can no longer eat my food. Joel frantically dials random telephone numbers. And James bolts for a neighbor's (any neighbor's) house.

"Our family is going to bond at the dinner table if it kills us all!" I vented my frustration one evening.

"That very well may be," John responded calmly.

"It could be worse." I retorted.

"Okay. You're right. We could live in a third world country. Mom, if you and Dad are so big on helping people discover what their purpose is in life, why don't you read the writing on the wall? A person who thinks vermicelli is an Italian composer does not have a purpose in the kitchen."

Harriet Nelson made it look so easy. She served a three-course meal every night at the same time—always hot I might add. Ozzie carved the meat and passed the plates with a silly grin on his face. David and Ricky came to the table impeccably dressed and never griped about green vegetables.

They make me sick.

If this is real life, what's a woman who experiences brain death upon entering the kitchen supposed to do? Throw myself across the bed and cry because my husband put the poison control number on auto-dial? Give up because the kids wear hard hats when I'm flipping pancakes? Walk out because the sanitation workers gave me my own toxic-waste container?

I'm tempted to say forget all you've been told about the family dinner hour. It's overrated. But don't think for a minute I have a bad attitude. I simply believe there are plenty of other times a family can connect relationally, communicate meaningfully, and make positive memories—such as taking long car trips together.

Truth be known, our first family vacation fourteen years ago left a lot to be desired—like tranquilizers. We never dreamed bonding could produce so much stress.

The night Bill asked if I'd like to take a trip to Colorado I was too excited to sleep. *Now's my chance to plan some family adventures our kids will always remember*, I thought.

Tossing and turning, I imagined the fun we'd have in the car during the peaceful eighteen-hour drive. We would stop to read historical markers along the road, discuss the changing scenery, and explore the rugged terrain on our journey—making the trip a stimulating educational adventure for our boys, then aged five and two.

Sometimes I amaze myself with my efficiency. I bought travel magazines, checked out books about traveling at the library, and requested free brochures from every Chamber of Commerce between my house and the Continental Divide. I mapped out our route and calculated to the mile where we'd stop to eat, sleep, buy gas, and use the restroom. My travel plans made Charles Kuralt look like an amateur of the road.

To tell you how much luggage and paraphernalia Bill packed per square inch into our so-called "family-size" car would have no meaning for anyone without a degree in physics. I'd like to attend the family reunion of the nincompoop from Detroit who invented the family-size sedan. He must come from a long line of trolls.

The photograph that sold us on this car showed a happy family of five cruising along an empty highway into the sunset. What the picture didn't indicate is that this family had no luggage, no pillows, no toys, no cooler of travel snacks, the mother is a petite fashion model, the father is a jockey, and the children's hands and ankles are bound and anchored to the floor so their bodies are moored exactly thirteen inches apart.

I ask you, are there no Boy Scouts in Detroit? Do car designers not know what it means for a family on vacation to "be prepared"? Granted, I may go a little overboard, but I think it's important to pack a *few* extra items so we can be ready for any occasion we might encounter. The way I see it, who knows when the governor of the state we're driving through might ask us to pop in for dinner. And it's important to feel comfortable in case we have an opportunity to attend an impromptu wedding, a costume party, a safari, a golf tournament, high tea, or an earthquake. I also like to pack enough medicine to treat every ailment known to humankind and enough food to get us through a month-long famine.

Actually, besides the neighborhood Fourth of July barbecue and the all-family ice cream social, watching Bill pack the car for our vacation ranks fairly high on the neighborhood top ten entertainment list. When he finally finishes packing, we crawl in bed with dreams of heading west, praying that the trunk will not explode before morning.

Call it a woman's intuition, but on this first family vacation when our two-year-old woke up on departure day with diarrhea, something told me we should have hired a sitter for the kids and booked a cruise. Since that trip, it has been my theory that parents who take small children on long car trips are half a bubble off plumb.

Why I thought two over-energized preschoolers would sit contentedly watching the scenery go by is beyond me. During the trip our backseat resembled a pinball machine as they bounced from one armrest to the other. Thirty minutes down the road I wanted to put the suitcases in the car and tie the kids to the luggage rack.

We learned quickly that little boys could care less about historical markers and geographical adventures. The only new territories they wanted to explore were expensive souvenir shops. By three o'clock the first day we'd managed to acquire a stuffed armadillo, an Indian headdress, and an "authentic" rubber Jim Bowie knife—all for a mere thirty-eight dollars. (And remember this was fourteen years ago when a dollar bought lunch, not a half cup of coffee.)

But that was only the beginning of our woes. After traveling for twelve hours we were exhausted. It was dark when we reached our en-route motel, so it was hard to tell if it looked like the picture on the brochure. The next morning we decided it probably did—thirty years ago.

When we opened the door to our "luxury" accommodations, Bill and I stared morosely at the sculptured velvet picture of Elvis hanging on the wall. As we unloaded, I was able to maturely deal with the sticky, matted shag carpet in our room. "We just won't take off our shoes," I said, trying to sound positive. And I felt some relief when Bill found our own can of roach spray in the closet. Actually, I didn't start crying until I pulled back the shower curtain and discovered why the place was called the Mason-Dixon Inn. Blue and gray mold was growing before my eyes.

"Things will look better tomorrow," I said hopefully.

They didn't. The next morning we invented the first "express checkout." On the way out of town we bought a can of disinfectant and stopped at a roadside park to sanitize our belongings. Now referred to as the Roach Motel, this became the first entry in my travel journal under the heading of places we never wanted to go again.

After nine potty stops, seven hours of whining, four packs of gum, three rounds of throw-up, two heated marital arguments, and a broken fan belt, we finally found the road to the "fabulous" dude ranch. Until that night, I had faith in our government's truth-in-advertising laws. I now have a greater appreciation for Ralph Nader.

Small wonder the brochure read *"Private* Western Paradise." It was fifty miles from nowhere. When we finally located the office, we expected to be cheerfully greeted by a staff of wranglers. Wrong—on two counts. Number one: The desk clerk made up the entire staff, and his idea of a cheerful greeting was asking for our credit card. Number two: Although he smelled like a barnyard, for some reason his tattoos and sleeveless t-shirt didn't fit your basic wrangler profile.

He turned off "The Dukes of Hazzard" long enough to find our reservation card and give us the key to Lookout Hacienda. Even though we were weary, just hearing that picturesque name reminded us of how much we had looked forward to our visit out West. Our vacation package promised a daily two-for-one breakfast buffet. The housing accommodations included a luxury two-bedroom, one bath guest house with a fully furnished kitchen, and a porch where we could enjoy watching the sun slowly drop in the western sky.

I may not be the most seasoned traveler, but I figured out early on there was a reason why this place was not recommended by AAA. The two-for-one breakfast buffet sounded like such a good deal. Too bad they didn't mention that "one" costs $12.95—a little steep for cornflakes. And saying the house had two bedrooms was a stretch—if you counted the large closet as a master bedroom and the living room/kitchen-turned-bedroom after 9:00 P.M. there were two. (They turned off the electricity at 9:00 so you could get the real feel of the old West.) The door to the master bedroom would close if we put all of our weight on the opposite side of the bed. And the bathroom was arranged so you could sit on the toilet, lean into the shower stall, and wash your hair at the same time. Pretty clever.

The "fully equipped" kitchen consisted of small refrigerator obviously left over from the Ice Age, a hot plate with two settings—cold and scorch, and a Dutch oven for cooking and doing laundry. The tiny cupboard stored two highball glasses, swizzle sticks, and a jigger. Finally, something useful.

Not only was the place small and ill-equipped, but it was also a black hole—sucking dollars from our wallets for items and services we thought were included in the price. Forget watching the sunset. The only thing we saw slowly dropping was our cash supply. After the third day we realized it was dangerously low. We figured there were two options. We could order water and grilled-cheese sandwiches at every meal or use a credit card to cover expenses. We chose the plastic. Five months at 18 percent of added interest later, our bill wasn't getting any smaller. We wanted to make lasting memories, but the bill for the "dud" ranch wasn't what we had in mind.

We learned a lot from our mistakes that year. We actually discovered that we love Colorado and that laughing at things we've endured together brings us closer together. And even though that particular location could use a little help—like from a pyromaniac—our family continues to vote for Colorado as our favorite place to vacation in the summer. For the past thirteen years we've driven eighteen hours and had a blast on the way. While there, we fish, hike, horseback ride, picnic, ride mountain bikes, and have our annual "blondes versus brunettes" spades tournament every night. Our family photo albums and hallways are filled with great memories from those trips.

Over the years, I've collected and cataloged a lot of helpful information about traveling as a family. Strange as it seems, I now write articles on this topic regularly and have included chapters on the subject in my other books. I may not be able to cook and sew, but I've got family car trips down to a fine art—except for one thing: the return home.

As far as I'm concerned, returning home is enough to make Norman Vincent Peale depressed. There are two main reasons for this feeling. First of all, we live in Texas. If you would like to experience what it's like to take a summer vacation in Colorado then come home to Texas, simply stand in front of an open deep-freeze for one minute. Then sprinkle yourself with water, turn your oven on broil, and stick your head in. If your scalp does not mildew in one minute, repeat the process.

Second, we have a house dog. Why, one might ask, would having a house dog cause depression at the end of a family vacation? If you have a house dog and you live in Texas, the answer to this question is obvious. Fleas.

Most people believe fleas are all alike. They are not. Texas fleas belong to gyms where they work out—which makes them bigger and stronger. They also have done extensive research in fertility and reproduction and have reduced their gestation period to three hours. I sincerely believe they have a plan to overthrow the state government and secede from the union.

Since a dog is like a biological magnet, when we leave town and leave our Border collie Charlie at the vet, the fleas lose their host and take over our home. They throw a house party and send out invitations to all the fleas in the neighborhood. Each year after vacation, we walk into the house with a positive attitude—hoping things will be different. It takes a few minutes to know if we have once again been overrun. Our big clue is when we look down at our pale ankles and they have turned black. Thus, our summer vacation ends with Flea Wars.

Bill, also known as Mr. Why-Pay-Someone-to-Do-It-Right, makes his annual trip to the chemical store our first day back home. He buys enough poison to kill every insect within a fifty-mile radius—and does just that—with the exception of our fleas, who wear gas masks. One hundred sixty-two dollars later he calls an exterminator.

Tell me I'm deranged, but I've never trusted an exterminator who sells burial plots on the side. It makes me wonder when he shows up wearing an astronaut suit and oxygen tank, then asks us to step out of the house for only five minutes. Anyway, the fleas disappear for a day or two—and so does another seventy-five dollars.

This past summer our fleas turned us into OSHA, so we decided to take a more natural, herbal approach. A friend who swore her dog never had fleas told me her secret: garlic pills. She said when the garlic gets into the dog's system and seeps out its pores, the fleas can't take the smell. Sounded good to me.

After a twenty-five-dollar trip to the health-food store and one week of hiding garlic pills in Vienna sausages, we noticed a difference. Our dog had gained five pounds and unbearably bad breath. The fleas hoisted an Italian flag and declared another victory in Flea Wars.

After fighting fleas, picking stale French fries from in between the seats of the car, and washing ten loads of clothes plus eight pounds of fool's gold left in the pockets, we get back to the daily grind. Our vacation is now a memory.

Memories. We talk about them as though we have a choice of whether or not to make them. We act as if the circumstances of life are like disappearing ink—only there for a moment. We forget our children's minds are like computer disks—constantly recording information. Who's to know which memories will be erased and which will be indelibly etched in their minds? Psychologists say it's the unusual or out-of-the-ordinary happenings—good and bad—that form the strongest memories. This means our kids won't remember how many shirts we ironed, how many deals we closed, or if the kitchen floor was mopped daily. But they'll remember the April Fool's Day we put an apple in their lunch with a gummy worm coming out of it. And they'll remember "Dress up Daddy" nights when he's their victim to dress up in crazy clothes or wrap up like a mummy in toilet paper. And they'll smile when they look at the photo album of the vacation when the whole family climbed a thirteen-thousand-foot peak together.

There's just something about being able to say, "Remember when. . . . That was hilarious!" or "This is the way our family always does it." Common experiences cement a family together. Every child's mind is a curator of memories. Fun family times and special traditions go a long way in building a rich museum of positive remembrances for our children.

In theory, most of us understand and believe this. But reality is another story—and time is the problem. Maybe you're reading this and thinking, "Humph . . . it's all I can do to get some semblance of dinner on the table at night—much less plan fun family activities and vacations. I'm exhausted." The fact is, many women feel the same way. The problem is widespread—and has serious implications. In *The Overworked American*, Harvard professor Juliet B. Schor reports that millions of women have fallen victim to the shortage of time.

> Women are coping with a double load—the traditional duties associated with home and children and their growing responsibility for earning a paycheck. With nearly two-thirds of adult women now employed, and a comparable fraction of mothers on the job, it's no surprise that many American women find themselves operating in overdrive. . . . They rise in the wee hours of the morning to begin the day with a few hours of laundry, cleaning, and other housework. Then they dress and feed the children and send them off to school. They themselves then travel to their jobs. The three-quarters of employed women with full-time positions then spend the next eight and a half hours in the workplace.
>
> At the end of the official workday, it's back to the "second shift"—the duties of housewife and mother. Grocery shopping, picking up the children, and cooking dinner take up the next few hours. After dinner there's clean-up, possibly some additional housework, and of course, more child care. Women describe themselves as "ragged," "bone-weary," "sinking in quicksand," and "busy every waking hour."[1]

Sound familiar? Read on. It gets worse.

Cross-cultural studies show that parents in the United States spend considerably less time with their children than almost any other country in the world. For example, although both Russian parents work and Russian children spend a great deal of time in family collectives, emotional ties between children and parents are stronger and the time spent together in meaningful ways is considerably greater than in the United States. Interestingly enough, the juvenile delinquency rate is much lower in Russia.

It ought not to be a surprise to anyone that kids equate how much we love them with how much time we spend with them. Time is a commodity item these days, but unlike money, everyone has the same amount. We spend it on what we think is important. Whenever I get too busy for my children, I remember the Lord Jesus. If there was ever a person who didn't have enough time, it was Jesus. He had to save the whole world in thirty-three years! And yet we read this interesting story in the Gospels:

> People were bringing little children to Jesus to have him touch them, but the disciples rebuked them. When Jesus saw this, he was indignant. He said to them, "Let the little children come to me, and do not hinder them, for the kingdom of God belongs to such as these. I tell you the truth, anyone who will not receive the kingdom of God like a little child will never enter it." And he took the children in his arms, and put his hands on them and blessed them. (Mark 10:13–16).

Children were important to the most important person in the universe, and he took time to be with them— much to the consternation of his disciples. In our adult world, it is easy to lose sight of what is really important.

Many of us feel guilty for not spending enough time doing fun things with our children or planning occasions for our family to enjoy together. We rationalize our feelings by taking sides in the quality time vs. quantity time argument. Those mothers who are adamant about spending small moments of "quality time" with their children usually do so in between meetings, appointments, or other "important" work. Sure, we may be playing a game or working on a creative project with our children, but they know when our minds are miles away. We can't fool our kids into thinking we're giving them focused attention.

Other moms are with their children for longer periods of time, but no significant bonding takes place. The mother is either dragging her child along on her errands or to her activities, or they're sitting in front of the television for hours together. We can be with our kids—without really being with them.

It's important to understand that quality time and quantity time are like the oxygen we breathe. Although the quality of the oxygen is important, the quantity determines whether we live or die. The same principle holds true in our families.

So what's a busy mother supposed to do? I'd like to make four recommendations. Please don't think these are mandates from "Mother Superior." They're simply principles that work for me.

1. Make relationships with your children a high priority. The good news here is that it's culturally "in" to do this. "In the nineties . . . kids are 'in' and the focus of life is on family and the home," said women's consumer trends expert and director of the Good Housekeeping Institute Amy Barr in a speech about women's trends. It's okay to jealously guard your time and "just say no" to people and organizations asking for your time—because you want to be with your children. Every need does not constitute an obligation. Remember, you're always saying "no" to something—try not to let it be time with your kids. And realize that climbing the career ladder and striving for individual status ultimately will prove empty and frustrating if gained at the sacrifice of family relationships.

2. *Schedule time each day to spend together as a family.* If possible, spend some of this time alone with each child focusing on his or her interests or needs. Nothing contributes more to the self-esteem of a child than your continuous and consistent emotional accessibility. If you work outside the home, use your lunch or break time to browse through activity and idea books for fun things to do with your kids that evening. I've found that if I don't think about what to do ahead of time, many times I'm out of energy and creative ideas by 7:00 P.M. When this happens, it's all too easy to capitulate to a regular nightly routine of watching meaningless television. If your job entails travel, call your kids at night to find out what happened in their world that day. Regular and consistent investments of time can yield great dividends.

3. *Encourage your organization or company to give high priority to the family.* Ask them to include families when planning conferences or conventions whenever possible. Request that they provide quality family-strengthening resources for their employees, and encourage them to create an atmosphere where employees can give family a prominent place in the promotion equation. Ask your company to consider giving employees permission to turn down promotions that require relocation that would uproot their family without being removed from their spot on the ladder. And ask them to consider providing excellent on-site child-care facilities for working mothers so they can spend time with their children during the day.

4. *Spend your money on making memories.* It's a good investment. If you have the choice of whether to take a family trip or buy a new piece of furniture, go for the trip. The furniture will get dirty, scratched, torn, and could end up some day in a garage sale. The family memory will last forever. Bill and I decided years ago that we'd rather our kids be raised in a house furnished in early garage sale—experiencing fun family memories—than a picture-perfect house full of expensive furniture with us never around.

Our children are growing up in fast and turbulent times. They need Home Sweet Home to be a place that offers plenty of time for recreation and renewal. As moms, we should regularly plan times for family fun, but it's easy to let days, weeks, even months slip by without making happy memories.

An economist has been defined as a person who knows the price of everything and the value of nothing. Maybe when it comes to spending time together as a family, we've become economists. We're keenly aware of the price of time—the extra income coming in with a second job and time-and-a-half paid for every hour of overtime. But perhaps we have forgotten the real worth of time—and what spending it with our children means in the long run.

Family Matters

Filling your children's minds with good memories takes some time and energy—not commodities already-tired mothers have in abundance. Sometimes a little encouragement or a fresh idea can get us over the hump and on the road to changes in our thinking and habits. Maybe something in the following list will do just that for you.

❧

Take time to evaluate how you spend your time. Record for two weeks how much time you spend with each child individually and together as a family in meaningfully relating. If you see it's not enough, schedule some memory-making activities on your calendar.

❧

"I'm constantly amazed by the number of people who can't seem to control their own schedules. Over the years, I've had many executives come to me and say with pride: 'Boy, last year I worked so hard that I didn't take any vacation.' It's actually nothing to be proud of. I always feel like responding, 'You dummy. You mean to tell me that you can take responsibility for an eighty million dollar project and you can't plan two weeks out of the year to go off with your family and have some fun?'"—Lee Iacocca in *Iacocca, An Autobiography*. Schedule a family vacation in advance. Planning can be part of the fun.

❧

Ask your child to make a list of his or her favorite five-minute, thirty-minute, and two-hour activities that you can do together. The list can be as long as you desire. Keep the list handy, and try to do at least two or three things a week. Depending on the child's age, the list might include:

Five-minute activities: Throw a football. Sit together and read a favorite book. Have a tickle war. Play a duet together on the piano. Play a game of hopscotch on the sidewalk.

Thirty-minute activities: Take a walk around the block. Work a crossword puzzle. Rearrange the furniture in his or her bedroom. Play a board game. Plan a party.

Two-hour activities: Go to the park for a picnic. Build a model. Go shopping. Go garage-saling. Go on a long bike hike.

❧

Find extra time to spend with your children by working smart. My favorite household administration book is *Mom's Little Instruction Book* by Rosemary Brown (Neat Ideas, Nashville).

❧

Turn an ordinary weekend into a holiday at home. Choose a weekend and put it on the calendar. Stock up on groceries and snacks. Get out board games and check for missing pieces. Rent a few family movies and pop some popcorn. Turn off your telephone and put a sign on your front door that your children can play *after* your holiday weekend. Keep chores and cooking to a minimum. Plan some Saturday outings everyone will enjoy. Go to church as a family Sunday morning then out for lunch. When you come home, your holiday will be over, but the memory of fun time spent just with each other will last a lifetime.

❧

Invest in a good camera, take a lot of family pictures, and put together photo albums. You'll be glad you did.

❧

When their children were young, one family started the tradition of taking a photograph of the state signs of every state they entered while on family vacations. Their goal is to collect photographs from all fifty states, place them in an album, and write special memories by each photograph.

૪ૐ

Good family memories occur when our activities revolve around something we all enjoy doing, helping individual family members achieve their full potential, accomplishing something through teamwork, and reaching out to friends.

૪ૐ

Spend time with your children by involving them in your work as much as possible. Take a child to the office once in a while or on a business trip.

૪ૐ

Plan a family reunion. When extended families get together, traditions are passed from generation to generation. It's good for kids to learn about their heritage. Plus, they'll have fond memories of meeting and playing with their cousins.

૪ૐ

"If a man insisted always on being serious, and never allowed himself a bit of fun and relaxation, he would go mad or become unstable without knowing it"—Herodotus. Give yourself the freedom to relax and have fun with your family.

૪ૐ

"That man is the richest whose pleasures are the cheapest"—Henry David Thoreau. Don't wait until you have a fat bank account to start making family memories because it might never happen. It doesn't take a lot of money to have fun together. Go on a family campout, take advantage of free community functions, plan an old-fashioned picnic.

ã

Don't stop making memories even though your child lives in a college dorm or apartment. Send a special care package for no reason except just to say "I love you."

ã

Don't allow televisions in your children's bedrooms. This promotes isolation from family activities.

ã

Create a family dream file. Clip articles and collect brochures of places you'd like to visit together. Work out a family savings plan or brainstorm about ways to earn extra money together.

ã

Listen to classic books on cassette while in the car or before bed at night. Experience the stories together.

ã

Remember the object of planning activities and occasions is to have fun and make memories. Part of the fun is being able to laugh with your family about your own flops.

ã

Take a vacation with a family with similar-age children whose company you enjoy.

ã

Make your mornings a time your kids will look back on a peaceful and positive time of family life. Mornings are the launching pad for your family's day. Organize your schedule so that you don't have to rush around, creating a stressful atmosphere. Your kids will have enough stress when they walk into school.

§₪

Volunteer for a worthy community project as a family, or adopt a needy person or family to help.

§₪

Look at the money you spend making memories as an important investment. A trip may be more important than new carpet.

§₪

Plan a meal everyone loves once a week and look forward to relaxing and enjoying it together—pancakes for Saturday breakfast, hamburgers for Friday night supper, Dad's chili on Sunday night.

§₪

Get involved in a hobby or project as a family—build a doghouse, have a family garage sale, train for a ten-kilometer run, breed and raise dogs, keep a giant jigsaw puzzle going.

§₪

Have a family ritual of tucking each child into bed every night—even when they are teenagers. When lights are out just before sleep is one of the most significant times for communication.

§₪

Create opportunities for your children to spend time with their grandparents. Research shows that it's through knowing our grandparents—or not knowing them—that we develop our attitudes about what it means to grow old.

Children who have little contact with grandparents are more likely to think of old people as frightening or strange, whereas children who spend time with grandparents see older people as kind and loving, with much to teach them. Make sure your children and your parents have ample opportunity to get to know each other.

&.

Give a copy of *Companies That Care* (Simon and Schuster/ Fireside, 1991) to your human resource department at work. It outlines the family services provided by more than one hundred companies that care about families.

&.

Bring back family dinner time. Eating together is an unparalleled opportunity for family discussion of issues both large and small. Encourage conversation by not allowing television and phone calls during dinner.

&.

Save memories of family trips by framing posters. The walls of our home are full of beautiful posters we picked up on family trips to Colorado and New Mexico. They not only make the rooms attractive, but serve as a constant reminder of the fun times we had together.

&.

Plan a surprise weekend for your family, and enjoy the pool, health club, and maid service at a local hotel. Many have inexpensive weekend packages that include breakfast. Play tourist in your own hometown. Take advantage of local attractions and events that you might not normally attend.

8

Family Finances, or How to Obtain a Loan Using Your Children as Collateral

*W*hen my banker learns I've written a chapter on family finance, he will no doubt call the Library of Congress to have this book reclassified as fiction. This guy has the personality of a bug zapper. To tell you the truth, I'm a little miffed at him at the moment. I think it's pretty tacky that some bankers send their customers discount interest incentives for new loans. And others give nice gifts for maintaining a minimum balance. My banker sends sympathy cards to my children.

I mean, the nerve of him to think I would overdraw my account on purpose just to aggravate his ulcer. I told him not to take it personally—that it's usually due to a simple addition or subtraction error, an automatic draft I didn't record, or the thirteen missing checks I forgot to enter in the checkbook.

But it still puzzles me how a person like me—who keeps impeccable records—could regularly be overdrawn. As soon as I write a check, I *immediately* grab a tube of lipstick or crayon and write down the approximate amount of the check on the back of a gum wrapper. And even if I do forget to record the amount of a check once in a while,

I don't worry about it because I keep a fifty-dollar buffer in the account to fool myself. This works well unless it's the check for the mortgage I forget to record.

Actually, I have my own method of accounting to balance our checkbook. I drop the last digit, add my weight (not the one on my physician's chart, but the one on my driver's license), multiply by the number of children under roof at that moment, and divide by my shoe size. That's close enough for me.

Those of you who relate in any way to this problem will have a greater appreciation when I tell you that after twenty-two years of traipsing bimonthly to the bank trying to prove my overdraft is a computer error—the greatest moment in my life finally happened. Forget the day of my marriage. Forget the birth of my children. Forget my books making the bestseller list. Forget being a guest on national television shows. Nothing, absolutely nothing, has brought me greater joy than the day I caught the bank in a $729 error *in my favor.*

Actually, I have made some progress toward keeping our checkbook balanced. I hired an accountant. But that didn't make figuring out our family budget any easier. Quite frankly, I think budgets are downright unbiblical. You probably already know this, but God did not create the budget. Nowhere in the Bible will you find God putting one of his prophets on a budget. No, God is a loving and generous God. The budget is a human idea.

But as much as I hate it, we need some sort of system to figure out how much money we don't have every month. No one has to tell me the national inflation index for me to know the cost of living is going up. Bill and James do a fair job of holding down spending, but in a family with two teenagers and a woman in midlife crisis, the overhead is pretty steep.

And to tell you how much it costs to keep my family of five fed would only make you think I'm a few shrimp short of a cocktail. I hate those women's magazines with articles about how to feed a family of six on ninety-six dollars a month. You show me a woman who can do this, and I'll show you a woman whose entire family is anorexic. The way my kids eat, ninety-six dollars gets me down the first aisle and halfway through the dairy case.

Since the cost of living seems to increase in our family by the hour, we've had to be creative about making extra money. One way we've increased our family income is buying houses, fixing them up, then selling them at a profit. But I must be truthful from the beginning and say if you don't have nerves of steel, a high threshold of pain, or a recent prescription for a sedative, this is probably not something you want to pursue. Yes, it's fun to work on projects together as a family. And yes, you can turn a nice profit. And yes, it can make you crazy.

The first stress-producing part of remodeling houses is applying for a loan. Few will argue that bankers consider those of us who fall into the dubious category of "self-employed" on the same level with lepers. If you're a person who believes in free enterprise, the American dream, or owning your own business, you might as well be under the death sentence. You have a better chance of getting a loan if you're unemployed, on welfare, and have no plans for the future.

During one particular house-hunting venture, we began our search for a home loan at a local bank. The loan officer looked like Ken—who had a wife at home named Barbie. He had perfect posture—so as not to wrinkle the back of his shirt, his nails were perfectly manicured, and he had a head of hair any televangelist would die for. But the hair on his neck was evidently not sprayed down, because it stood straight up when we mentioned we were self-employed. We didn't stay long.

Our second appointment was at a mortgage company whose president met us at the door to shake our hands. This guy wore a polyester leisure suit reminiscent of the 1970s and had one very long hair he wrapped around his head like a turban. He didn't look like a financial kind of a guy, but we were desperate for a loan so we followed him into his office. He asked about the home we'd like to buy and slipped a pen into Bill's hand while spreading an array of documents in front of us.

"If you'll just sign the loan agreement," he said, "we can get on with the minor details of the arrangement."

I envisioned myself hanging pictures over the fireplace and sitting with the children in front of a cozy fire.

"Where do we sign?" I commented anxiously.

"Not so fast," Bill responded cautiously.

Upon learning the exorbitant interest rate and huge down payment his company required, my dreams turned to sitting in front of a campfire outside the tent we'd be living in. We later learned not only was his appearance bogus, so were his loans.

Our third appointment was with a loan officer at a large bank. We were relieved when he didn't seem bothered we were self-employed. I breathed a sigh of relief when he said he wanted to work with us. We started the loan application process.

It didn't take long to figure out the word *privacy* had absolutely no meaning to this man. He wanted to know everything from our blood type and underwear size to how many times we brush our teeth each day. He called us every day for the next three weeks to ask more questions. I had to account for every penny I'd spent for the past three years. Trust me, this was no small task for a woman who uses her canceled checks for confetti on New Year's Eve. Feeling a little put out, I suggested to Bill we just take off our clothes and stand in front of his desk. He knew every other detail of our lives—why not all?

In what was obviously a great act of faith on the banker's part, he loaned us the money for the house we wanted to remodel. But you must understand that families like ours, who don't have a lot of extra capital to invest, must live in their house and work on it at the same time. This can be interesting—to say the least. We discovered that "before and after" pictures in home remodeling magazines are a bit misleading—because they don't show the in-between stages. Think about it. Have you ever seen a picture of a woman shaving her legs with a paring knife over the kitchen sink because the bathroom's torn up? Or how many photographs show an irate lady trying to track down the electrician, who skipped the country after installing her ceiling fan with two speeds—off and hurricane? And, I ask you, how many magazines do you know that would feature a candid shot of a wife slipping a mickey into her husband's coffee because the dishwasher he installed goes through the dry cycle first? Obviously none. Small wonder the home-remodeling business is a great income producer for marriage counselors as well.

Just last year we made our seventh move in twenty-two years. This experience qualified us to be the poster family for a local psychiatric hospital.

First of all, after remodeling our last house, we lived in it for eleven years. This posed a definite problem for a woman who lives with four men who refuse to throw away their old toothbrushes. The square footage shrunk, the closets disappeared, and we could not find the garage.

"If we're going to put our house on the market, we'll have to clear a path so lookers can walk through," I said with authority.

They did not respond. I knew I'd have to be ruthless.

"Okay, boys, let's start with your things," I said. "I think we can probably live without this headless G.I. Joe figure . . ."

"No way you're throwing him away. He's my favorite guy," James countered.

"Fine. How about this stringless guitar? It's just taking up space."

"Don't touch my guitar!" Joel pleaded. "In five years I'm going to start my own band."

"Well, surely you can live without this box of dead tennis balls."

"Mom, don't touch our stuff," John begged. "When you run an ad for the house, just don't include our room. That way, when we move out and the new people move in, they'll think they got a bonus room with the deal."

I knew at this moment that moving would not be easy. I would have to clean out clutter incognito.

I want to insert here that I try—with God's help—to be a woman who always tells the truth. I've taught my children that half-truths or not speaking up when asked a question to which they know the answer is the same as telling a lie. With every one of you reading my book as my witness, I confess that when my teenagers asked if I had seen their collection of 538 bottle caps, I said I gave them to a man who came to the door holding a gun and wearing pantyhose over his head. When James couldn't find his treasure box filled with three years' worth of expired toy coupons, a paper-clip necklace, fourteen empty fast-food containers, an empty jelly packet, and seven jelly-coated pennies, I told him I had no idea where it was.

(Well, I didn't have any idea which garbage dump it ended up in.) And to this day, when Bill asks me if I've seen his very favorite faded, stained, shabby, ragged, bedraggled, dilapidated work shorts, I quickly change the subject.

Once I cleaned out enough clutter so we could honestly advertise that the house had closets, it went on the market. For a woman whose kitchen is listed on Club Medfly's most desirable list, keeping things public-ready is no party. We asked our real estate agent to put "Call before showing" in our ad, so at least we could hide the breakfast dishes in the clothes dryer before people walked through. We learned that most agents did call—from their car phones in front of our house. Good thing the house sold in three weeks because we couldn't live life in fast-forward much longer without becoming the first family to suffer simultaneous coronaries. I'm telling you, when the phone rang we moved at the speed of light. We put dirty clothes under potted plants, threw wet towels in the deep freeze, and hid newspapers in the piano. When we moved, I found my checkbook in the waffle iron.

After signing away our valuables, any possible inheritance, and our children at the title company we started loading up our belongings. Our first trip over to our new house, I gathered from the look on a neighbor's face that most families move their belongings in moving vans. We resembled the road crew from Ringling Brothers Circus. It took three days, but we finally got everything moved— and we saved a lot of money moving ourselves.

Exhausted, we sat down in a circle of odd pieces of furniture and dedicated our house to God. We prayed that he would make it a home filled with love, joy, and good memories. I personally prayed that if any family member ever mentioned the idea of stretching our budget by remodeling and moving again, God would keep me from wringing their neck.

Quite frankly, I don't know of too many families who aren't always on the lookout for ways to stretch their budget. Not having enough money to make ends meet can cause a lot of stress. But as strange as it seems, so can having more than enough money. One day I received phone calls from two friends—both upset over money problems. One was feeling down because her husband's business had "gone south" and she didn't know how she was going to pay the bills. She said they were at each other's throats constantly because of the financial strain. The other friend shared with me she was angry with her husband because he wouldn't let her touch their three-hundred-thousand-dollar nest egg. He made her scrimp and save—very rarely allowing their family to spend money on anything fun.

Whether the problem is too much or too little, our society and the media make it difficult to avoid materialistic attitudes. It's even harder to teach our kids a healthy perspective about wealth. Wearing the right clothes, driving the right car, living in the right neighborhood seems essential for acceptance these days. Being a recovering materialist myself, I know this is a real uphill battle.

Coming from a family with a strong work ethic, I grew up thinking that money was the result of hard work. So if I wanted more, all I had to do was work a little harder or smarter. But there was a whole new factor I had to learn. Although God wants me to work hard, the good things in life are a gift from him. James reminds us, "Every good and perfect gift is from above, coming down from the Father of heavenly lights, who does not change like shifting shadows" (James 1:17).

In an industrialized nation it's easy to begin to believe that whatever we have is solely a result of our performance.

In an agrarian society, people understand how dependent they are on the things only God controls—rain and sunshine for example. The thought that you can work yourself to death and have calamitous climatic conditions that ruin your crop tends to make a person more dependent on God. It's obvious to all of us that a farmer who doesn't acknowledge God as his partner is a presumptuous fool. Yet when it comes to the business world, the direct tie to nature is broken and the constant reminder of dependence on God is dimmed.

Attitude Adjustments

If I want the best for my children, it is obvious that a correct view of material possessions must permeate my thinking and attitudes. Paul gives some great advice to his young friend Timothy:

> Do you want to be truly rich? You already are if you are happy and good. After all, we didn't bring any money with us when we came into the world, and we can't carry away a single penny when we die. So we should be well satisfied without money if we have enough food and clothing. But people who long to be rich soon begin to do all kinds of wrong things to get money, things that hurt them and make them evil-minded and finally send them to hell itself. For the love of money is the first step toward all kinds of sin. Some people have even turned away from God because of their love for it, and as a result have pierced themselves with many sorrows. . . .
> Tell those who are rich not to be proud and not to trust in their money, which will soon be gone, but their pride and trust should be in the living God who always richly gives us all we need for our enjoyment.

Tell them to use their money to do good. They should
be rich in good works and should give happily to
those in need, always being ready to share with others whatever God has given them. By doing this they
will be storing up real treasure for themselves in
heaven—it is the only safe investment for eternity!
And they will be living a fruitful Christian life down
here as well. (1 Tim. 6:6–10, 17–19 TLB)

Like any of God's gifts, wealth can be used or abused.
I see three dangers and three blessings of wealth in these
verses we should be aware of ourselves and should teach
our children.

The Dangers of Material Wealth

Material wealth can make us proud. Arrogance has
been a classic problem of the "haves" ever since there were
"have nots." I often hear critical remarks by those who are
affluent about those who are not as prosperous. Evidently
this is not just a problem of the twentieth century. In the
1800s George MacDonald wrote:

There is scarce a money-making man who does not
believe poverty the cousin, if not the child, of fault.
Few who are themselves permitted to be financially
successful realize that it may be the will of God that
other men should be, in that way unsuccessful, so
that better men can be made of them in the end.[1]

But thinking critically about wealth—or lack
thereof—is not limited to the rich. I'm sad to say that some
of the most critical people I know are those who have less
than others. Out of jealousy, they judge the motives and
spending habits of those who have more. Unfortunately,

money is how we keep score in America. And if we're not careful, wherever we find ourselves on the societal pecking order we'll be tempted to look down on or uppity at those who have less or more than we do—and we'll pass this prejudice on to our children.

One of the strongest trends in America today is called "entitlement." People have come to believe that they "deserve" a certain lifestyle. From my limited experience, it seems as though people who think they deserve something seldom do. If we have any degree of prosperity, we should be thankful. It's not because we deserve it, but because God has given it to us as an act of grace. That doesn't leave much room for arrogance.

Material wealth can make you independent. Usually independence is good—unless it is from something essential to life. For example, if you declare your independence from oxygen, we can predict your soon departure. Money can make us think we're self-sufficient and powerful—that we can take care of ourselves. An independent mindset causes us to have the attitude, "Who needs God—or anyone else for that matter?" Paul warned Timothy, "Tell those who are rich not to be proud and not to trust in their money."

Not only is it stupid to trust in material wealth, but as many of our friends in the oil business found out a few years ago, it is spiritual suicide. Illusions that we can take care of ourselves are just that: illusions. There are incredible factors totally beyond our control that affect our ultimate welfare. Solomon, the richest and perhaps most powerful man of his time, wrote:

> Unless the LORD builds the house,
> They labor in vain who build it;
> Unless the LORD guards the city,

The watchman keeps awake in vain.
It is vain to rise up early,
To retire late,
To eat the bread of painful labors;
For He gives to His beloved even in his sleep.
(Ps. 127:1–2 NASB)

We can waste our lives on seeking more. The problem of focusing on material wealth is that there is never enough. Someone asked Rockefeller how much would be enough. He said, "Just a little more." No matter how rich we are, if we love money there will never be enough. Material possessions simply cannot satisfy the soul of man. Only God can meet our deepest longings. Trying to replace him with things results in, as Paul said, many piercing sorrows. Not only do we perpetuate our emptiness by not seeking God, but we tend to use people and destroy those relationships as well.

Last year a large corporation offered me a job that paid extremely well. The day before I was scheduled to fly to the corporate headquarters to discuss the details of the job and to give them my decision, we had a time of family prayer. It's funny how a large sum of money can drastically improve your discernment about what God's will is. The boys began dreaming of shiny new sports cars—obviously gifts from God. Equally as seduced, Bill and I fantasized about purchasing things from the "want column" of our prayer list as we rationalized how the large amount of time I had to commit wouldn't affect family relationships.

The following day while sitting at a long mahogany table with company executives, I came to my senses. I realized this job would mean a lot of financial freedom for our family, but this freedom would come at a high cost. It would cost huge amounts of time away from my family—possibly jeopardizing those relationships—and it would cost getting sidetracked from what I believe to be my God-given passion of helping busy women strengthen their families. In a rare moment of wisdom, I turned down the job.

The Blessings of Material Wealth

Of course, there *are* many advantages of wealth—if we don't let it consume us. *Material wealth provides wonderful opportunities for personal growth and development for ourselves and our family.* If you think God has a problem with money, look again at 1 Tim. 6:17 (TLB): God, "who always *richly* gives us all we need for our *enjoyment.*" Whatever God has given to you, be it great or small, use it and enjoy it. God is not utilitarian.

Material wealth provides opportunities to do good things for others. Paul said, "Tell them to use their money to do good" (1 Tim. 6:18 TLB). Whether it is sponsoring a worthy cause, providing for someone else's needs, or simply sharing God's goodness with others, God intended his gifts to be used, not simply accumulated.

Material wealth can create eternal treasure. Paul said, "By doing this they will be storing up real treasure for themselves in heaven" (1 Tim. 6:19 TLB). When we recognize that everything we have is a gift from God, when we manage it well and use it wisely and generously, we please our Master. Being a generous God, he opens even more treasure to us as faithful servants—treasure that is safe from thieves, inflation, and taxes.

If we want to teach our children a biblical view of material wealth, we need to begin with our own attitudes. Acknowledge God's sovereignty over your finances. If you are struggling to make ends meet, ask God to provide for your needs and to guide you to the opportunities he has for you. If you inherited wealth, thank God and acknowledge him as its primary source, and thank him for the hard work of those who went before you. If God has prospered you through hard work, thank him for the abilities and opportunities he has given you—without which you would be destitute. If there is money in the bank, acknowledge God as the source of your security, not your bank account.

Obviously if wealth comes from God, then I am accountable to him for what I do with it. That means that I need to develop an attitude of gratitude for all I have and give him the ownership. My children need to see this attitude in me. When I want something, do I rush out and buy it or stop to consider: Is this the best use of my money? Is this what God would have me do?

What Kids Need to Know about Material Wealth

When there is not enough money for what I want, do my children see me griping or praying? Am I able to be content with what God has given me, or am I always wanting more?

Actions must follow attitudes. Many parents I know have what seems to be a godly attitude toward material wealth, but they fail to communicate their philosophy to their children. Communication needs to be both verbal and action oriented.

Children need to understand two crucial things: First, they are not entitled to everything they want. Second, they will not get everything they want. We live in an area where parents lavish gifts on their children. Without realizing it, well-meaning parents turn their children into Cornucopia Kids.

Dr. Bruce Baldwin, psychologist and author, defines a Cornucopia Kid as "a child who grows up with the expectation, based on years of direct experience in the home, that the good life will always be available for the asking without the need to develop personal accountability or achievement motivation." Parents' material well-being can be extremely detrimental to children's maturation into emotionally healthy and responsible adults. He lists ten questionable parental behaviors that help create Cornucopia Kids.

1. Your child's room is filled virtually to over-flowing with toys and other fun things because you know your neighbor's children have the same.

2. You consistently give in to your child's demands for more things after only token resistance.

3. Your child starts many new projects or hobbies, but then loses interest and never follows through to completion.

4. You help your child excessively with homework and other school projects.

5. Your child gets all the latest "fad" items shortly after they hit the market.

6. With your help, your child always has unearned money available for spending.

7. You threaten your child with punishment for breaking rules or other infractions, but you hardly ever follow through.

8. You often jump to protect your child from directly experiencing the consequences of inappropriate behavior.

9. Your child frequently responds to you with rude disrespect, and good manners are not demanded at all times.

10. You permit your children to watch a great deal of television daily, even on school days, because then the kids do not bother you.[2]

Wealth must be handled with wisdom. If we're not careful, it will possess us, rather than us it. Thomas Carlyle said, "For every one hundred men who can stand adversity, there is only one man who can stand prosperity." Jesus had the same message for the rich young ruler: "It is almost impossible for a rich man to get into the Kingdom of Heaven" (Matt. 19:23 TLB).

It's a blessing from God to have money and the things it can buy. We just need to be careful to make sure we don't lose the things that money can't buy.

Family Matters

The privilege of having money brings great responsibility. One of the most important aspects of our children's education is a healthy perspective about money and material possessions—and they won't learn that at school. Our homes must be the classrooms. Use the following ideas to check the emphasis of your curriculum.

ف

Do your children think invention is the mother of necessity? Instant gratification—without the need to save or sacrifice—has become a common way of life in America. Buying the latest clothes, electronic games, or sports equipment as soon as they hit the market is unhealthy. If your kids badly want something like this, let them earn money to pay for half of it, and you pay for the other half. They'll appreciate it more and take better care of it.

৯৯

"The greatest use of life is to spend it for something that will outlast it"—William James. On what are you spending your life and your resources?

৯৯

Don't get caught in the trap of spending money on your children to ease your guilt of not spending enough time with them.

৯৯

"Few rich men own their own property. The property owns them"—Robert G. Ingersoll. What does this quote mean to you?

৯৯

Teach your kids that privilege brings responsibility. Let them experience the consequences of irresponsibility. If a child leaves his bike outside instead of putting it in the garage, and it is stolen, he earns the money for a new one. If a teenager gets a speeding ticket, she pays for the ticket and the increase on the insurance bill.

৯৯

"Where your treasure is, there your heart will be also" (Matt. 6:21). We know where our treasure is by what we spend our money and our time on.

৯৯

Let your teenager help you pay your monthly bills. At age seventeen, John's job became to write the payee and the amounts on the checks, then Bill or I would sign the check and record the amount. This was an eye-opening experience for John about the cost of living. As a result, he became much more frugal.

ॐ

"Beware of little expenses. A small leak will sink a great ship"—Benjamin Franklin. Work as a family on your spending habits. Identify any small leaks and plug the holes.

ॐ

"When I fed them, they were satisfied; / when they were satisfied, they became proud; / then they forgot me" (Hos. 13:6). If you have been abundantly blessed with material possessions, acknowledge regularly as a family the source of your blessings that you might not forget God.

ॐ

Make sure your children feel good about themselves on the inside—then they won't depend on money or possessions for their self-esteem.

ॐ

"You never know what is enough unless you know what is more than enough"—William Blake. Determine how much is enough for your family.

ॐ

"Content lodges oftener in cottages than palaces"—Thomas Fuller. I know wealthy people who are miserable and people who live with little who are extremely happy—and vice versa. The source of their feelings of security and significance make the difference. If it comes from wealth and possessions they will never be happy. Work on adapting the attitude that if it comes from God, you will have joy in plenty or in want.

❧

"What shall it profit a man, if he shall gain the whole world, and lose his own soul?" (Mark 8:36 KJV). Evaluate how much you work and what it's worth to you and your family.

❧

Use everything you have as if it belongs to God. It does. You are his steward.

❧

Never forget that your posterity is more important than your prosperity.

❧

"Put in its proper place, money is not man's enemy, not his undoing, nor his master. It is his servant, and it must be made to serve him well"—Henry C. Alexander. Talk together as a family about how money serves you.

❧

Never do anything or buy anything on a regular basis for your children that they are capable of doing or buying for themselves. Your role as a mother is to help them become independent, self-sufficient adults.

❧

Poverty in its truest sense is a child who gets everything he wants; has a closet full of clothes but still doesn't have a thing to wear; spends money on perfume, makeup, jewelry, and designer clothes—and still worries about her image; has a closet full of games or toys—and still has nothing to do; has so many things on his want list, he doesn't have any money to help others. Work with your children to make realistic lists of their needs and wants. And encourage them to feel "rich" in helping others.

ॐ

Create opportunities for your children to earn their own money. Encourage them to work and save money for things they dream about.

ॐ

"We make a living by what we get, but we make a life by what we give"—Winston Churchill. Talk about what you give as a family.

ॐ

Open a checking account for your teenager. Set up a budget and help her learn to manage her own money.

ॐ

"He that trustest in his riches shall fall" (Prov. 24:28 KJV). What are you trusting in?

ॐ

"Prosperity knits a man to the world. He feels that he is 'finding his place in it,' while really it is finding its place in him"—C. S. Lewis. Can you relate to these words?

ॐ

"I have learned the secret of being content in any and every situation, whether well fed or hungry, whether living in plenty or in want. I can do all things through him

[Christ] who gives me strength" (Phil. 4:12–13). If my children witness this attitude in me, chances are good it will rub off on them. Unfortunately the converse is also true. If my children have an attitude problem, I need to examine my own as well.

🙖

"There is nothing so habit-forming as money"—Don Marquis. Do you or your children have some bad spending habits that are causing your family financial stress? Shopping and spending money can become an addiction.

🙖

"For of those to whom much is given, much is required"—John F. Kennedy. Sit down as a family and talk about what you can do with your material resources to make the world a better place.

🙖

Teach your children that God is the source of everything we have. Although we work and earn money, unless he gives us air to breathe and our bodies and minds to use, we would have nothing.

🙖

If you were suddenly blessed with wealth, do you know how you would react? How would your priorities change?

🙖

Include your children in family financial discussions in age-appropriate ways. In a financial crisis, make sure your children don't feel as though they are burdens. When cutbacks are necessary, try to see that they affect family members fairly.

9

The Stomach Virus and Other Forms of Family Bonding

No one has to tell me when the stomach virus will make its annual debut in our family. The same package arrives year after year. Only the name of the carrier and the arrival date change.

The night James reports in vivid detail at the dinner table how Mary Elizabeth hurled "chunks" all over his spelling paper right before show and tell I know it's a matter of about thirty-three hours before the virus hits our house. I'm usually right to within an hour.

I keep hoping medical researchers will discover some sort of over-the-counter remedy that will disable the virus once a person has been exposed. Perhaps a way to mainline virus-smart medical missiles. Or maybe an industrial-strength enema that disinfects while it cleans. Or the answer might be an eighty-proof gargle. If it doesn't kill the germs, at least you won't care if you're sick!

Until these products are available, I will continue to expect the same predictable scenario. James will shuffle swiftly down the hall to our bedroom in the middle of the night. He will stand by *my* side of the bed, wake *me* up, and tell *me* he needs to throw up. He knows he'd need a bullhorn and a cattle prod to get his father's attention.

After James announces his intention to throw up, he indeed does just that—usually about seven feet in front of the toilet. More times than not, it's my luck we had chili or spaghetti for dinner.

The ruckus awakens the older boys, and they crawl out of bed to see this thing that has come to pass (excuse the expression).

"It doesn't look much different to me than it did at dinner," John comments under his breath.

"Nice shot, James," Joel adds. "Haven't you ever heard of the gag rule? The idea is to hit the toilet. This is sick."

"Brilliant deduction," I respond flatly. "I suggest you stop breathing unless you want to be next."

I spend the next twenty-four hours giving James clear liquids and helping him deal with the tyranny of the urgent—whether to sit down or stand up in the bathroom.

The older boys are the next victims. Within forty-eight hours one is hugging the toilet. Twenty-four hours later, the other one follows suit.

Two days later, it's Bill's turn.

I'd like to insert here that in many families, fathers and mothers experience various types of role reversals. On the whole, it's usually the mother who cleans and bandages the wounds, administers the medicine, and nurses the patients back to health. In our family, the opposite is true. Next to Kathy Bates, I'm the last person you want for a nurse. I cringe at the thought of an open wound, become nauseated at the sight of blood, and have been known to stick the wrong kind of thermometer in the wrong opening. (I'll leave that one to your imagination.)

When Bill gets sick, to say his life is in danger is an understatement. Somehow, though, he always manages to nurse himself back to health. Then the inevitable happens. I get a whiff of someone's peanut-butter sandwich and bolt for the bathroom.

It's funny about the stomach virus. It completely changes my values. When I'm in good health, I have to force myself to take aspirin. Simple, over-the-counter drugs make me feel like my elevator is stuck between floors. Since I want to run my home and business to the best of my ability, I take as few drugs as possible. But give me the stomach virus, and I'll fork over my sterling, my frequent-flyer miles, and my children (not necessarily in that order) in exchange for drugs. Shoot me up with *any-thing.* Just put me out of my misery until it passes.

Overall, it takes about eight days total for the virus to run its course through our family.

Since I'm one who likes to make the best use of my time, I always thought it would be much more efficient if our entire family had the stomach virus at the same time—getting it over with in one fell swoop. Like a lot of things that sound great in theory, though, reality is a different story.

One particular winter, dream became reality. Our entire family lay motionless on our king-size bed—moaning when someone had to run to the bathroom. The phone rang. No one moved. The doorbell rang. No one moved. The dog whined to go outside. No one moved. When the mattress swayed, it felt like a raft in the middle of the South Pacific. As waves of nausea hit us simultaneously, we realized we had a big problem. There weren't enough bathrooms to go around.

"Someone's got to make their way into the kitchen to get the antinausea suppositories out of the refrigerator," Bill managed to mutter.

"I'd rather die," John moaned.

"You may get your wish," Bill responded without glee. "We'll probably all die of dehydration before the evening news if we don't get the suppositories."

No one volunteered.

"Okay, I'll get the suppositories, then we'll all insert one at the same time," I said faintly. "Just think—this will be a great family memory. I wish I had the strength to find the camera."

"You're sicker than I thought," Bill gasped and headed for the bathroom.

So much for time management. But who knows how much significant bonding took place around the toilet that day? Difficult circumstances are like that. It's hard to see the good until you're on the other side.

I believe it's true that a family can grow stronger during hard times. But it can also grow apart. Many times a mother's attitude makes the difference. I learned this principle by watching the responses of a woman in a community where we once lived.

Sally and Richard (not their real names) had been married for twenty years. Richard worked his way up the career ladder to become vice president of a large corporation. Because of his generous salary, they lived in a lovely home, drove late-model cars, and traveled extensively. Their children attended the best private school. They were sailing smoothly through life—when all of a sudden the bottom fell out. Very innocently, Richard made a poor judgment call about a business deal and someone in the company falsely accused him of criminal activity. He lost his job.

The top-notch attorney they needed to bring the truth of his innocence to light cost them their savings. They were able to keep their home, but Sally had to give up her car—not to mention the lifestyle to which she was accustomed.

Instead of becoming angry, she responded in love and support. She got a job and led the children to rally around Richard during subsequent months when he fell into a deep depression—which made things even harder. But Sally never stopped praising him to the children.

Years later, they both admit the situation was extremely difficult. But they're thankful it happened because of what they learned and for what it did in a positive way for their family. Today, Sally and Richard work at their own company, which they built together from scratch when they were forced to start over.

I asked Sally how such hard circumstances served to bond their family closer together. She answered openly and said, "I tried to never forget that 'family' is what's important." She went on to say she tried to remember their family is more important than bank accounts, material possessions, and what people said.

God created the family to work as a unit, so we can give one another support and learn to love each other during the good times—as well as the bad. Sally's attitude made her calamity a success story.

I know another woman who experienced similar circumstances and also started over—but in a different way. She packed her bags and walked. Actually, adverse conditions that might be classified as failures are what drive many women to harbor resentment and bitterness. Unwilling to forgive, their conditional love causes a rift or even a breakup of their family.

The family is the place where we learn that life can always be counted on to be hard and that people will always let us down. It is also the training center for learning how to love and how to express love. Love is the basic attitude the Bible gives concerning human relationships. We are to love our neighbors, our parents, our spouses, our children, and even our enemies.

If we have the attitude "perfection or nothing" about human relationships, we can count on ending up with nothing. No one has a perfect family situation and no individual family member is without fault. I think this is what Paul was referring to in 1 Corinthians 13:4. To say "Love is patient, love is kind," implies that there are probably some things about which it would be easy to be impatient and unkind. For instance, some kids with selective hearing and memory problems can't hear you when you ask them to remove their wet towels from the dining-room furniture and can't remember from one day to the next that wet towels will spot wood. But they can hear you from around the block when you whisper that it might be fun to go swimming this evening and remember that three weeks ago you said you'd take them and then didn't. Another example is the spouse with a degree in engineering who can follow complex blueprints for a multimillion-dollar office complex but can't follow simple instructions for boiling pasta. Or we're impatient and unkind ourselves when we're so tired we respond in anger to a hurt child. The list is endless. We all have irritating habits, weaknesses, or failures.

Refusing to forgive and overlook shortcomings or failures is the quickest way to destroy any family relationship. When we dwell on a person's negative character traits, it's easy to forget the wonderful things we love about him or her.

Paul went on to say love "does not envy, it does not boast, it is not proud. It is not rude, it is not self-seeking, it is not easily angered, it keeps no record of wrongs." If you, like me, had a Pollyanna paradigm going into marriage and family life, you've no doubt been disappointed.

Who hasn't been tempted to feel jealous when a husband would rather play golf, go fishing, or is forced to work overtime? Who hasn't taken that as a sign: *He doesn't love me.* Who hasn't been tempted, when a child says she can't run the washing machine, to arrogantly respond, "Why when I was your age I washed the whole family's laundry in a tub then hung it out to dry with my bare hands in twenty-below-zero weather"? Who hasn't been tempted to bring up that time when our feelings were hurt—twenty years ago.

It didn't take me long to figure out that loving other human beings on a day-to-day, hour-to-hour basis is hard, self-sacrificial work. It's a lot easier for me to think arrogant, if-only-he-were-like-me thoughts. Embarrassingly, feeling provoked to anger comes quite naturally for me. And some days, keeping score of Bill and the boys' offenses is second nature. But I know that real love must shower a lot of grace and forgive again and again.

Paul undoubtedly knew this because he also wrote, love "always protects, always trusts, always hopes, always perseveres. Love *never* fails" in weakness and failure, when our suspicions have been right, when the bank account is empty, and when we're overwhelmingly disappointed. Love says "I'll always be here for you." Love keeps the door open, dinner in the oven, and the porch light burning—for years and years.

In truth, it's not the easy situations that bring out the depth of our love, but the difficult ones. Love grows and bonding occurs when we accept each other "as is," bear one another's burdens, stand together in the face of failure or rejection, and support each other during catastrophes such as illnesses, financial setbacks, loss of job, poor cooking . . . whatever!

To do this means we must have a positive attitude in the midst of negative circumstances. This is a constant battle for me, but I've discovered when I remember three things, the fight is easier.

1. *The problems I would like to escape from are the very things God wants me to face and grow from.* Whether the situation is an outside crisis, like being laid off, or a personality clash within the family, the first thing I need to realize is that it is no accident. If my goal is the immediate relief of pain, then bailing out makes a lot of sense—so does heroin. If, however, I want to see the bigger picture, I must realize that painful situations are part of God's curriculum for my life. It is here that God works to make me like Christ from the inside out.

Avoiding pain guarantees a shallow life. But facing pain and seeking to grow from it develops character. In Romans 5:3–5 the apostle Paul wrote,

> We can rejoice, too, when we run into problems and trials for we know that they are good for us— they help us learn to be patient. And patience develops strength of character in us and helps us trust God more each time we use it until finally our hope and faith are strong and steady. (TLB)

The fact is that God's agenda for us is bigger than we ever dreamed. We're not talking about a minor remodeling job, but a total transformation. His plan—past, present, and future—is to make us like Christ. C. S. Lewis put it like this in *Mere Christianity:*

I think that many of us, when Christ has enabled us to overcome one or two sins that were an obvious nuisance, are inclined to feel (though we do not put it into words) that we are now good enough. He has done all we wanted him to do, and we should be obliged if he would leave us alone.

But the question is not what we intend ourselves to be, but what he intends us to be when he made us. . . .

Imagine yourself as a living house. God comes in to rebuild that house. At first, perhaps, you can understand what he is doing. He is getting the drains right and stopping the leaks in the roof and so on: you knew that those jobs needed doing and so you are not surprised. But presently he starts knocking the house about in a way that hurts abominably and does not seem to make sense. What on earth is he up to? The explanation is that he is building quite a different house from the one you thought of—throwing out a new wing here, putting on an extra floor there, running up towers, making courtyards. You thought you were going to be made into a decent little cottage: but he is building a palace. He intends to come and live in it himself.[1]

2. *I come to know God in a way I could not understand apart from pain.* In Ephesians 3:17–19 Paul wrote,

And I pray that Christ will be more and more at home in your hearts, living within you as you trust in him. May your roots go down deep into the soil of God's marvelous love; and may you be able to feel and understand, as all God's children should, how long, how wide, how deep, and how high his love really is; and to experience this love for yourselves, though it is so great that you will never see the end of it or fully

know or understand it. And so at last you will be
filled up with God himself. (TLB)

I discover the height of God's love on the
mountaintops. But I discover the depth of his love in the
valleys of life. When I look back over the past twenty-six
years of my relationship with God, I must honestly confess
that the major growth spurts of my character have come as
a result of allowing God to take me through hard situations. Although I've fretted and fussed over marital dis-
cord, friends who let me down, difficult job situations,
financial setbacks, illnesses and surgeries *ad nauseam,* I see
how God used these situations to build my character. Although I don't wish difficult circumstances on myself or
anyone else, I now don't expect life to be free from pain,
one delightful day after another, because I know I still
have a lot of growing to do.

**3. *My lack of joy in a difficult circumstance cannot
be blamed on my circumstances or on someone else.*** Joy is
my choice. The older I get the more I realize how little control I have over life's circumstances—and other people.
But I do have control over my attitude. The minute I start
blaming my bad attitude on Bill's insensitivity, a child's
disappointing me, or a business associate's offending me,
I am off-base. God has given my attitude a declaration of
independence. In John 14:27, Jesus told his disciples,
"Peace I leave with you; my peace I give you. I do not give
to you as the world gives. Do not let your hearts be
troubled and do not be afraid." While Paul was in prison
he was able to write, "Rejoice in the Lord always, I will say
it again: Rejoice!" (Phil. 4:4).

All right, already, I know it's a cliché. But I don't think
anyone has invented a better metaphor for this principle

than the half-empty glass versus the half-full glass. If our glass of life is half-empty, we're never going to have enough—time, money, love, sweet memories. We're always in danger of running out. And we surely aren't going to recognize peace in our lives when it presents itself. We're too busy worrying that somebody—not ourselves surely—is going to tip over our glass.

If our glass is half-full, on the other hand, there's something left for us. We don't have the perfection of a full glass, yet we've got half a glass, and it's always there. Perhaps we lose a home, a job, have a sick child, or endure pain and suffering. But God is always there, making sure the glass is never empty, and at least half-full of joy and peace.

God gives us the peace that passes understanding. We are human. We can't understand why some things happen to us. We can't understand why, after we work so hard and feel we deserve a break, someone else, who seemingly doesn't lift a finger, is showered with blessings. We can't rationalize our way to perfection. We can accept his peace—which helps us see our circumstances from a positive perspective.

In a family, a positive perspective brings incredible interpersonal effects. It looks for the good. It eliminates the necessity of critical remarks and manipulative behavior. Since these tactics don't work anyway, I do myself (and others) a favor when I give up my compulsion to concentrate on what's wrong, changing and blaming everyone else. That's not my job. My job is to focus on my attitude.

And when I have a positive attitude, I create an incredible opportunity to affirm my love for my family. In the midst of their failures and shortcomings, God wants them to feel his love. My ability to forgive, forget, and love despite their faults sends a powerful message of not only my love, but God's as well.

Family Matters

I've often wished for a place where I could get an attitude overhaul—a place where I could take myself, like I take my car when the engine needs work, and someone would painlessly do the necessary adjustments and replacements in about eight hours. Then I could pay them and come home good as new. The truth is, there is a way to get an attitude overhaul. But more often than not, it's painful, it usually takes more than eight hours, and it comes with a price—a high price to many of us. It costs us our pride. We have to stop blaming others or God for our problems and allow him to renew our minds and change our perspectives.

Maybe one or two of the following ideas will encourage you to allow God to begin an attitude overhaul about some things you're struggling with.

❧

"In adversity remember to keep an even mind"—Horace. These words are pretty easy to remember—when you're not in crisis. Try to remember them when you are.

❧

Good music soothes our souls and brings peace to our minds. Collect inspirational music and play it often.

❧

"Nobody, who has not been in the interior of a family, can say what the difficulties of any individual of that family may be"—Jane Austin. It's easy to look at others and think their lives are perfect and that we're the only one who suffers. That's simply not true.

&

"Two can accomplish more than twice as much as one, for the results can be much better. If one falls, the other pulls him up; but if a man falls when he is alone, he's in trouble" (Eccles. 4:9–10 TLB). When a family member is going through a hard time, don't make it worse by putting him or her down. Go through it together.

&

"God is our refuge and strength, / an ever-present help in trouble" (Ps. 46:1). Spend time daily reading God's Word and praying.

&

"A friend loveth at all times, and a brother is born for adversity" (Prov. 17:17 KJV). Don't try to go through hard times alone. Let down your guard and let someone else share your burden.

&

"I gain strength, courage and confidence by every experience in which I must stop and look fear in the face . . . I say to myself, I've lived through this and can take the next thing that comes along. . . . We must do the things we think we cannot do"—Eleanor Roosevelt. If a difficult experience has paralyzed you, take a small step toward the thing you think you cannot do.

&

"Who has never tasted what is bitter does not know what is sweet"—German proverb. If you're going through something hard, take a moment and write down your blessings. Chances are you'll notice new things.

≈

"The best thing about the future is that it comes only one day at a time"—Abraham Lincoln. Live one day at a time.

≈

"In times like these, it helps to recall that there have always been times like these"—Paul Harvey. Take time to recall.

≈

"Is any one of you in trouble? He should pray" (James 5:13). Act on these words often.

≈

Pain and hardship will either make us bitter or better. The choice is up to us.

≈

Let God make you a strong person. "Strong people are made by opposition like kites that go up against the wind"—Frank Harris.

≈

Think about this: "Let nothing disturb you, let nothing frighten you: everything passes away except God; God alone is sufficient"—St. Theresa.

≈

"Boys, this is only a game. But it's like life in that you will be dealt some bad hands. Take each hand, good or bad, and don't whine and complain, but play it out. If you're man enough to do that, God will help and you will come out well"—Dwight D. Eisenhower, quoting his mother. Children aren't the only ones who whine. We would do well to regularly ask ourselves if we're whining about the cards we've been dealt.

§a.

Get involved in a share group with people of like-minded values. We all need a support group of friends.

§a.

"You will keep in perfect peace / him whose mind is steadfast, / because he trusts in you" (Isa. 26:3). Meditate on God and his Word when you are in pain.

§a.

My neighbor Holly Howard has an incredibly positive attitude about life although she lost her leg in a boating accident. Instead of becoming bitter over her loss, she prayed that God would help her concentrate on what she did have.

§a.

Sometimes when we're dealing with a hard situation, it's easy to get an I-don't-care-about-anything attitude. This is a good way to make matters worse. Take good care of your body when you're under stress. Exercise regularly, eat wisely, and get plenty of rest.

§a.

"Adversity reveals genius, prosperity conceals it"— Horace. Some of the greatest ideas and breakthroughs in our family have come during the toughest times. Look for solutions together as a family.

۶۰

Robert Louis Stevenson said, "Go on in fortune and misfortune like a clock in a thunderstorm." One of our family expressions we use when under duress is, "We've gotta keep on keepin' on."

۶۰

"The mind is its own place, and in itself can make a heaven of hell, a hell of heaven"—John Milton. My frame of mind is up to me.

۶۰

Plan something fun to do. Get your mind off your problems.

۶۰

Whenever I get into a negative frame of mind and begin to gripe and complain, I try to see myself in the future—how I want to have responded to the situation. I don't want to be a negative person.

۶۰

"Let us be of good cheer, however, remembering that the misfortunes hardest to bear are those which never come"—James Russell Lowell. Don't spoil the gift of today by worrying about tomorrow.

۶۰

"Whoever is happy will make others happy too. He who has courage and faith will never perish in misery." Collect quotes you want to describe you. I want this quote by Anne Frank to describe me as a mother.

Never forget that God will never give you more than you can bear. (See 1 Corinthians 10:13.)

10

If Home Is Where the Heart Is—
Perhaps We Need a Bypass

The greatest thing a mother can do for her children is love their father. And vice versa. For years, this adage has been quoted, painted on plaques, and carved into paperweights. I for one believe there's some truth to this principle.

I don't want any recognition or awards, but let it be known that I try to love my husband and be a good wife. To do this, gracious person that I am, I've had to overlook a lot of things in my twenty-two-year marriage to Bill.

I've overlooked his climate eccentricities. When Bill ordered an electric blanket the night we checked into our honeymoon suite—the last day of July—I should have known what kind of life I was destined to lead. Frankly, I think all premarital counselors should administer a climate-compatibility test to every engaged couple. Forget the personality inventory tests that measure whether you're an introvert or an extrovert, passive or aggressive, and intuitive or pragmatic. This information is utterly useless when it comes to arguing over temperature. I think it's more important for a wife to understand from the beginning that her husband's feet turn to blocks of ice when the temperature goes below fifty. And a husband, on the other hand, would surely benefit from knowing his wife's idea of a cool breeze is North Dakota during a January Winnipeg Clipper gale.

Over the years we've learned to compromise. On the nights when Bill sets the thermostat to somewhere between *Some Like It Hot* and *Backdraft*, I simply open the windows. When I turn on the air conditioner in December and begin humming "Let it snow, let it snow, let it snow," that's his cue to put on long underwear, turtleneck sweater, and wool socks.

I've also overlooked his recurring bad dreams about someone chasing and attacking him. Call me nonsensual, but my idea of intimate bedfellows is not being kicked in the midriff in the middle of the night. After his last bad dream, which of course he slept through like a baby, I woke him up.

"Excuse me," I tapped him on the shoulder, "but I didn't realize I was sleeping with Steven Seagal. Would you mind telling me who it is you're fighting off? I just want to know if it's worth my turning black and blue."

"Look," he replied, his eyes opened half-mast, "just cool your jets and be thankful you're not married to that guy I counseled last year who dreamed about water skiing. His wife's had back trouble ever since he used her as a slalom ski and made it twice around the lake. Go back to sleep."

And I've overlooked the ponderously slow way he makes decisions. I have never been your basically patient person. So when I ask Bill if he wants spaghetti for dinner and he has to mull it over, write out the pros and cons, check to see if it fits into his life blueprint, and pray about it, I start feeling a little testy. I decide it might be quicker to order in—from Sicily. Ask if he wants regular or creamy Italian dressing on his salad and I pull up a chair to get comfortable.

If we need to make a big decision—like buying a car—I prepare to grow old. I will never need a copy of *Consumer Reports*. Bill methodically takes his time and collects answers to questions about cars the editors never dreamed of asking. The man becomes a walking automotive encyclopedia. On the other hand, when I think about buying a car, I only want to know two important facts: What color is it and will I look cute driving it?

I've also overlooked the fact that he is incredibly easy to please. Strange as it seems, it gets on my nerves that I rarely have anything to get mad at him about. In my mind, people need a little conflict every once in a while to keep life interesting. Sometimes I try to get a rise out of him by preparing the three foods he detests—tuna casserole, cooked carrots, and green peas—all at the same time. He merely smiles and gives thanks that at least he has food to eat. Or once I facetiously told him I wanted to watch "Recycling Bat Guano" on television, which happened to be at the same time as the Cowboys' playoff game. He responded calmly and told me he'd always wanted to learn more about bat guano. It's nauseating.

But when I really get desperate for some relational adventure, I know the ultimate ticket. I drive his car—with him in it. To a deeply spiritual man, a woman who strips gears, lays rubber, and makes road pizza out of squirrels is definitely a test of his endurance. I'm not saying how frustrated he gets, but when's the last time you met a man who'd rather walk five miles on broken glass than ride with his wife?

In truth, Bill and I really are about as opposite as two people can be. I'm just thankful he's not writing a book entitled *Do Divorce Lawyers Take Visa?* The things Bill has had to overlook about me could, of course, be jotted down on a matchbook, a matchbook the size of the Empire State

Building. He could, no doubt, write a substantial chapter about the trials and tribulations of living with a woman who never knows how much food is in the pantry, how much money is in the bank, and how much gas is in the car. (Usually they're all empty.)

Yes, Bill and I have put in quite a bit of conflict-resolution time over the years, but we've also experienced unspeakable joy. We see each other as an invaluable blessing when we realize our differences give us a breadth and depth to our relationship we wouldn't have if we were alike. Then there are the times we've come to an impasse in our relationship and wonder how we'll ever resolve it. We look at each other and shake our heads in despair. When this happens, we count the possible cost of our feelings. Remembering our marriage vows did not include an exit clause and that we're committed to giving our children our best, we stick with it until the problem is solved. This takes time, patience, and faith.

Most child-rearing experts agree that the husband-wife relationship is the most important relationship in the family. Both the quality of the parent-child relationship and the child's security are largely dependent on the quality and depth of the marital relationship.

Although healthy families are not free of conflict, research has shown that in successful families who raise healthy kids, the parents have a deep intimacy with one another. This intimacy gives them a reservoir of strength they can draw from to help them cope with problems and resolve conflicts.

When we hear the word *intimacy*, we usually think of two things—physical closeness and emotional transparency. Intimacy, however, involves more than that. It encompasses our entire being—mind, emotions, body, and spirit. God designed us to share our lives on these four planes. Like anything worthwhile, intimacy takes work, time, and commitment.

Mental intimacy is the meeting and merging of two minds based on mutual respect. I'm not implying that a couple must agree on every point, but rather a common understanding and esteeming of each other's ideas, thoughts, and values. It does imply that two people have come together on the major issues of life.

Mental intimacy is built on communication. One reason why so few couples communicate is because they've let other commitments and activities crowd their schedule. They have no time for each other. Sometimes Bill and I get so busy we have to schedule an appointment or set aside a block of designated time to spend with each other. This may seem a little extreme, but our busy careers and our children's schedules devour any one-on-one time with each other. Years ago when we felt estrangement creeping into our relationship, we cut back drastically on the amount of television we watched. Suddenly we had more time to talk and really listen to one another. We can't grow mentally intimate unless we learn what the other thinks and feels about issues.

If you feel a need to work on this aspect of your relationship, you might start by reading a book together, studying an issue, or undertaking a project that requires you to exchange ideas. Bill and I try to find out what we can learn from each other, and we don't let pride, intellectual arrogance, or criticism hinder us. We just enjoy the process of growing intellectually together.

Emotional intimacy is the meeting and merging of two emotional beings based on mutual openness. Emotional intimacy moves beyond opinions—to deep feelings.

It develops in an atmosphere of understanding and trust as two people share their dreams, fears, experiences, and secrets with one another.

Women, as a whole, seem to have a much easier time communicating their feelings than men. It's threatening for many men to let down their guards long enough to let someone see into their vulnerable inner person. That's why emotional intimacy grows only in a place of safety. Building trust creates an atmosphere conducive for this level of communication to take place. Criticism, nagging, and anger all stunt the growth of emotional intimacy. No one wants to communicate his or her feelings to someone who is constantly on the offensive. Instead, we must learn to listen carefully and compassionately whenever our mates reveal how they feel—without judging. Solomon said, "The purposes of a man's heart are deep waters, / but a man of understanding draws them out" (Prov. 20:5).

Emotional intimacy has a vocabulary of its own—made up of words of praise, encouragement, and understanding. This is the language of love. Speak it frequently and you'll notice emotional oneness developing.

Physical intimacy is much more than great sex. It's a warm, touching relationship based on mutual affection. Every person needs the physical touch of other living beings. We all have a deep-seated hunger for the concrete reality of human contact. Warm, physical affection that is not necessarily a prelude to sex is basic to love and intimacy. Every couple we've ever counseled stopped touching before they stopped caring.

Next time you go to a movie, take a lesson from the teenagers. They hold hands. They snuggle up next to each other. They sit so close their silhouette looks like a two-headed monster. If we're not careful, we old married folks can sit on opposite sides of the car, sleep on opposite sides of the bed, and eat on opposite sides of the table—growing farther apart as the years go by.

Try to start the habit of touching your mate every chance you get. Not as a signal for "I'm ready," but simply as an expression of your affection. I've heard many women complain, "The only time he touches me is when he is ready to make love." If this is a problem, talk about it with your spouse. Be specific about when, where, and how you want to be touched. And be patient if one partner is more affectionate than the other.

Spiritual intimacy is sharing our spiritual journey based on a mutual dependence on God to meet our deepest longings. Spiritual intimacy provides the atmosphere to share our deepest thoughts about God and the struggles and joys we have in becoming what he wants us to be.

Spiritual intimacy begins with a personal relationship with God and the belief that he absolutely accepts and loves us as we are through Christ's death—which paid the penalty for our sins. Our new forgiven position gives us the freedom to give, encourage, and serve our mates rather than demanding that they make us absolutely secure. It gives us both the freedom to soar in our relationship when we are aware of God's constant presence in our lives. This gives us the spiritual resources to weather the storms when marriage is less than we hoped and life is harder than we can handle alone.

Perhaps the easiest way to begin your pilgrimage of spiritual intimacy is regularly reading together. Read a passage from the Bible, a chapter from a good book, or a devotional guide—then talk about your insights. Get up early and begin your day together or try it just before you go to bed. Listen to tapes in the car together and discuss what you learned.

But the strongest way to build spiritual intimacy is to pray together. Exchange prayer requests so you can pray during the day for each other, and try to spend at least a few minutes praying aloud together.

Be aware that pushiness can hinder an atmosphere of mutual spiritual growth. Be patient and understanding, and take it slowly if need be. Make sure your desire for spiritual intimacy doesn't drive your husband away. The reward of your effort here will mean a deeper level of intimacy on all levels of your relationship.

A dear friend—I'll call her Betsy—began her own personal spiritual pilgrimage ten years after reading the book of John. She oozed with excitement over her new-found understanding of God's love for her and what it meant to become his child. She wanted this for her husband Tom too!

Because Tom had no interest whatsoever in spiritual matters, her zeal completely turned him off—and even made him angry. Their marriage deteriorated to the point where they lived under the same roof, but that was all they shared.

On the brink of divorce, she prayed and searched her Bible for help. First Peter 3:1–2 seemed as though it was written personally to her:

> Wives, fit in with your husbands' plans; for then if they refuse to listen when you talk to them about the Lord, they will be won by your respectful, pure behavior. Your godly lives will speak to them better than any words. (TLB)

That day Becky felt impressed to never talk about spiritual things with Tom again—unless he brought up the subject. She also decided to strive to be an excellent wife by living out her beliefs daily.

That was three years ago. Today their relationship is better than ever. Tom still does not have a personal relationship with God, but he's much more open and inquisitive about spiritual matters—and the seeds of spiritual intimacy are beginning to take root. Becky patiently prays for Tom every day.

Intimacy between husband and wife helps bind a family together. It gives children a sense of security. It also gives children a healthy model to follow when they grow up and have their own families.

However, it is a reality in our culture that not every child will grow up with both parents living in the home in a happy and fully intimate marriage. Many books have been written on the subject, and I in no way claim to be an expert. I do know, though, from talking with friends and from years of working with women from a variety of backgrounds that you don't have to have two present parents to have a happy and healthy home or to give your children a sense of security, in short, to do your job as a mom.

I've seen people who divorced and used their children as pawns for their continuing battles. I've seen families in which the father has totally disappeared, and the mother has used that sad fact to color the whole way she relates to her children. "Life is insecure," she might as well be whispering into their ears all night long, every night. She shows them in many little ways that they can't rely on anyone, that they won't be taken care of.

And I've seen the exact opposite. I've seen divorced spouses pull together as a parenting team better than they ever did when they were married. I've seen abandoned women pull their lives together and teach their children lessons about going forward with courage in the face of adversity.

If you're a single mom and have lost your husband to death, undoubtedly yours is a difficult road to travel. If you're a single, divorced mom, you've got a different difficult road. But in either case, you're still a mother. And your concerns, worries, and rewards are pretty much the same as any other mother's. And, like other mothers, a lot of what happens in your family depends on your attitude.

You can't develop an intimate relationship with a husband you don't have. You can, however, care for yourself in a deeply intimate way. You can do yourself and your kids the favor of taking care of your own needs for mental, emotional, physical, and spiritual intimacy. Not all of anybody's intimate relationships are with a husband or with any one person. We all have somebody—mother, father, siblings, our college roommate, the friend we met fifteen years ago—with whom we can develop various aspects of an intimate relationship.

Developing mental intimacy with yourself might mean taking the time to read new books, go to lectures, and take the time to just sit with yourself quietly to clarify your thinking. It might mean joining a book-reading group or a parents' discussion group.

Developing emotional intimacy might mean meeting with a good friend just to talk about how things are going for each of you. It might mean seeing a counselor who can provide a safe place for you to get comfortable with your feelings. It might mean letting your children know how you feel—not what you think, but how you feel.

Developing physical intimacy doesn't mean I'm advocating having one, or a number, or a series of sexual relationships. But I do suggest that you can cultivate friendships. You can open yourself to hugging and being hugged by friends and family, demonstrating to your children that there's such a thing as nonsexual touching. You can take care of your body, perhaps eating right and exercising, and modeling for your children that you—and they—are people worth caring for.

Developing spiritually, of course, begins with God. And God wants us to have a relationship with him whether we're married or not. We don't have to check a "married" box on any sort of application to be valuable in his eyes. Perhaps your developing spiritual intimacy will lead you to join a Bible study group or a prayer chain. Perhaps you can feel comfortable asking others to remember you specifically in their prayers and offer to do the same. And surely you can pray with your children daily.

In short, from other relationships you can get much of the support you need. And you can model intimate relationships for your children.

Developing those relationships can do three things. It can make you a healthier, happier, less resentful mom. It can teach your kids the value of getting close to people in their lives. And it can help you resist the urge to invest all you need for closeness in your children, to use them as surrogate spouses in your life, and to try to live through them.

Maybe you feel as though your family could use a bypass—a way to get around difficulties, a way to get through to others, a way to find the center of your heart, a way to draw strength from God and each other. Developing intimacy can help you do just that.

Family Matters

We live in a world where "cocooning" is in. People are hunkering down, holing up, drawing their shades, and burrowing in. These are not actions or attitudes that promote intimacy—between spouses, children, neighbors, whomever. As it is with most things worth having, if we want intimate relationships, a fulfilling life, and a happy home we must be willing to risk and to work. I encourage you to use some of the following ideas to begin a pilgrimage of developing intimacy in your own family.

🙶

Make a list of things you like about your husband. Concentrate on these things—not the things that drive you crazy. The size of our character is often measured by the size of the things that get our goat. The conquest of petty irritations is vital to the development of intimacy.

🙶

Marriage is not expecting my husband, nor myself, to be perfect. It is cultivating flexibility, patience, understanding and a sense of humor. It is our giving each other an atmosphere in which we can grow.

🙶

Read a good book with your husband or a close friend and discuss it.

🙶

"Mid pleasures and palaces though we may roam, / Be it ever so humble, there's no place like home"—John Howard Payne. How does your family feel about your home?

🙶

Create an atmosphere in your home where family members know it's okay to cry. Cry with your children about something they feel hurt over, and let them see you cry when you're hurting. This promotes intimacy and healthy expression of our God-given human feelings.

"Victory is not won in miles but in inches. Win a little now, hold your ground, and later win a little more"—Louis L'Amour. Usually relationships don't change overnight. Be patient with the person you're trying to develop intimacy with.

The key to all successful relationships is self-esteem. Schedule some time each week to take care of yourself—physically, intellectually, socially, and spiritually.

Let your kids see you reaching out and caring for your adult friends who are going through a difficult time.

Read the Bible with your husband. Or pick up a devotional guide at your local Christian bookstore to give you some initial guidance.

Plan a weekend retreat for you and your husband. Getting away—just the two of you—is good for your children as well as for your marriage.

"I am only one; but still I am one. I cannot do everything, but still I can do something; I will not refuse to do the something I can do"—Helen Keller. If you are the only person in your family committed to promoting intimacy, don't give up. You don't know what good your efforts may do.

§ふ

Turn off the television and talk about something other than the leaky faucet, what's on sale, and what you had for lunch.

§ふ

Read a weekly news magazine together and discuss an article or world event.

§ふ

Talk openly with your husband about how you like and don't like to be touched. Respect each other's feelings.

§ふ

If you're a single mom, get together with other families on a regular basis, not to demonstrate to your children what a "real family" looks like, but to let them experience the intimacy of an extended family. This could be your own blood relatives or close friends.

§ふ

Work on a picture album together or look back through an old one. Ask your husband how he felt at different occasions as you view the photographs.

§ふ

Taking care of yourself—getting exercise, pursuing interests, eating right—demonstrates to your kids that you are somebody worth caring for and so are they. For more ideas about how to get on the road to becoming your best self, read my book *Do Plastic Surgeons Take Visa? and Other Confessions of a Desperate Woman* (Word Publishing, 1992).

૱

Watch old home movies as a family. Take turns providing commentary about your lives growing up.

૱

Tell your children what you like about their father.

૱

Attend church or a Bible study together. Discuss what you learned.

૱

"Character calls forth character"—Goethe. Your life makes a difference—in your relationship with your husband, as well as your children.

૱

If your husband is not interested in spiritual things, ask yourself what there is about your life that would attract him to God.

૱

"Progress always involves risk; you can't steal second base and keep your foot on first"—Frederick Wilcox. What does this mean in your life?

૱

Pray together regularly. Bill and I are committed to praying together daily, but with our busy schedules, unfortunately, we forget. Sometimes we let days go by without praying together—and our feelings of spiritual intimacy wane. Instead of getting down on ourselves for being irresponsible, we simply remind ourselves of Matthew 18:19–20 and get back on track. "Again, I tell you that if two of you on earth agree about anything you ask for, it will be done for you by my Father in heaven. For where two or three come together in my name, there am I with them."

&

Find a positive support group of friends. Don't hang around people who constantly gripe about their lives.

&

"Be angry, and yet do not sin; do not let the sun go down on your anger" (Eph. 4:26 NASB). Finish arguments *before* you go to bed—even if it means staying up until the wee hours of the morning.

&

"A quarrelsome wife is like a constant dripping" (Prov. 19:13). Be a gracious person. If you and your husband are at each other's throat—habitually arguing about trivial things, make your motto "Don't sweat the small stuff." Everyone living under your roof will be happier.

&

"A happy mother makes a happy child"—anonymous. Don't neglect caring for your children at the expense of caring for yourself. You'll be a better mother if you take care of yourself personally.

&

Depending on your children's age, talk honestly with them about why you and their dad no longer live together as husband and wife if that is your situation. Make sure they understand it is not their fault.

৪•

If you're a single mom, don't try to make your kids your whole life. Get involved in a church activity, a parent-support group, or simply go to dinner with a friend.

৪•

Develop a positive attitude toward your own body. Meditate on Psalm 139:14–16. You are a one-of-a-kind work of art.

৪•

"The wise woman builds her house, / but with her own hands the foolish one tears hers down" (Prov. 14:1). Do something today to build your house.

৪•

If you are a single mom, try to find positive male role models for your kids. Nobody can be a substitute for their father, but a loving uncle or friend can provide them with male companionship.

৪•

"It is a rough road that leads to the heights of greatness"—Lucius Annaeus Seneca. When striving for intimacy in a relationship produces pain, which it often does, remember intimacy is a great endeavor.

৪•

"Charm is deceptive, and beauty is fleeting; / but a woman who fears the Lord is to be praised" (Prov. 31:30). Sit down alone and spend some time evaluating your life.

Ask yourself how your family would describe you. What attitudes and habits could you change that might make your home a happier place and a woman "to be praised"?

"Submit to one another out of reverence for Christ" (Eph. 5:21). Talk about what this verse means in your marriage.

Talk with your older children about your hopes and dreams for them regarding family intimacy and how those might differ from what you experienced. You can be honest about your own feelings without "dragging out the dirty laundry" or complaining about how hard your life was or is.

11

Does God Answer 911?

$\mathcal{W}$e have become a nation of people who hate to ask for help—myself included. I strongly believe the airline industry—among others—is to blame. Thanks to the airlines, asking for help has become a very unpleasant experience.

It has to be a reasonably good day—meaning the children sleep until afternoon, I receive an income-tax refund, or I see a photo of an old high-school rival who now weighs twenty pounds more than I do—before I'll dial to request help with flight information. It takes every ounce of courage I can muster to remain calm when the direct-dial system answers.

"Hello, and welcome to Mosquito Republic Airlines. In order to *expedite your call* (if that's not an oxymoron, I'm a natural blonde) please make your selection from the following menu:

"If you want ticket information to cities beginning with the letters A through J that have a population of less than seventy-five thousand, press one. We don't have flights to any of these cities, but press one anyway. This will connect you to another recording with information concerning cities to which we do fly.

"To receive incorrect flight arrival and departure information about domestic flights, press two. To receive correct information, proceed to the airport and wait for the plane.

"To book a free flight using bonus-mile coupons, press three—then wire the phone to your ear so you can accomplish something while you wait—like working a five-thousand-piece jigsaw puzzle or spring cleaning your house.

"To book a full-fare, first-class flight, press four. An agent will be with you in three seconds.

"Press five if you wish to file a complaint concerning airport security because a man wearing a ski mask, carrying a Saturday-night special in one hand and a bag of a white powdery substance in the other breezed right through security while they frisked you and disassembled your curling iron in search of drugs.

"To request nutritional information about in-flight meals, press six. This will connect you directly to Poison Control.

"If you're feeling stressed-out and want travel information about our relaxing resorts, punch in your credit card number and throw the phone against the wall."

One day after a frustrating attempt to ask an agent for help, it occurred to me that I'm really glad God doesn't use a Dial-a-Prayer automated answering system. Think about it. What if you prayed and got an answer like this:

"Hello. We're glad you called heaven. At the present, God is busy, but the first available angel will be with you momentarily. Please do not hang up."

After a harp duet of "I Need Thee Every Hour," you hear: "Thank you for holding. If you would like to speak with someone about a minor miracle, press one.

"To be connected to the major-miracle department, press two—then make your selection from the following menu:

"For financial calamity, press three, your checking account number, and the date of your last deposit.

"If you have severe health problems, press four and the first three letters of your disease.

"For protection while traveling, press five and the airport code of your destination.

"If you have marriage problems, press six and the date of your wedding.

"For help raising children and managing your family, please leave a message on God's voice mail. He will get back with you as soon as possible."

Quite frankly, if God worked like that I'd be in deep trouble. My questions and frustrations about motherhood alone are enough to warrant a direct line to heaven. I need a lot of help—on a daily basis.

I started this book on the premise that being a mother and running a family is a very big job. After washing five loads of clothes, listening to four seven-year-olds run through the house, making trips to the grocery store, the orthodontist, the cleaners, the library, and the post office, attending a basketball team parents' meeting, and cleaning up a large deposit of dog poop, I have not changed my mind. Family management in and of itself is a full-time job, and I think a lot of people are waking up to this issue. An interesting speaking request confirmed this paradigm shift to me.

Because I write books, and my books have either a picture of me or my entire family on the back, sometimes I get calls from public relations firms who are looking for a spokesperson with a "mom" image. They usually want me to endorse a product or be a part of a family-image campaign for a corporation. I enjoy doing this kind of work if it doesn't take too much time away from my family and if the product is something I feel comfortable endorsing.

This past spring a PR firm contacted me in search of a spokesmom for a certain corporation, whose name they could not disclose at first. They had chosen ten women from across the nation as possibilities for this spokesmom position. For three months I mailed biographical information, books, magazine articles, photographs, and tapes from television programs to the PR firm at their request. Finally, they called to tell me they had narrowed down the field to two finalists—one of whom was me. They also told me the spokesmom they chose would be representing a well-known hair-care products company. When I relayed this information to my children, they almost hyperventilated with hysteria.

"Hair products!" Joel caught his breath as he bent over double in laughter, "Mom, do you actually believe this company would choose someone whose hair looks like they comb it with a spaghetti server? I don't think so."

"Who's the other candidate," John chimed in sarcastically, "Lassie's mother?"

"You think you're funny don't you?" I retorted. "If I'm chosen, don't come begging for me to share my fee with you."

As it happens, I was chosen. And not because of my hairdo—or lack of one. The company was not looking for a woman to do hair-products commercials. They were looking for someone to be part of a public relations program to inform consumers that their company was interested in and wanted to offer help in other areas of their lives, not just hair care. I was chosen to give a speech to the editors of major women's magazines on the subject of family management and how a woman can have a career, be a good mother, and run her home efficiently at the same time.

"So what's so profound about that?" you ask.

There's a lot that's profound about that—and I'll tell you why.

In the seventies and eighties, many colleges and universities conveyed the notion that the role of mother was passé, and women who settled for such a role—and nothing else—were settling for second-class citizenship. Many women did not feel free to choose a career as a full-time mother and homemaker without apologizing for their decision. Unless they pursued a career in addition to raising children, they considered their lives a failure. This degraded the position and role of mother and homemaker. Family was just not a priority.

Not any more. Although today's family may not resemble the Cleaver household, many of the values from the fifties are resurfacing in the nineties. Many sources agree.

- Dr. Jack Lessinger, author and professor emeritus at the University of Washington, predicts "as we approach the 21st century Americans will continue looking for ways to lay aside acquisitive consumerism for *new priorities of family life and home.*"

- In their recently released book, *Megatrends for Women,* Patricia Aburdene and John Naisbitt state, "The 1990s mark a new phase in family history, a turning point: *people are finally beginning to revalue and again appreciate the importance of the family.* A wealth of studies [and] polls . . . show a family revival is getting established. Many parents who may have overworked in recent years now want to change: time off work to spend time with family is emerging as the *status symbol* of the 1990s."

- "Eight out of ten Americans declared that they would sacrifice career advancement in order to spend more time with their families. . . . A majority of Americans report that they are willing to *relinquish even current income to gain more family and personal time,*" according to *The Overworked American* by Juliet B. Schor.

- *Time* magazine reported that Americans are looking for a standard of living that can't be measured solely in dollars and cents. We are *hungry for safe, sane lives, strong families, love, commitment, and values.*

Family Circle magazine, where I am a contributing editor, underscores this trend every time I receive a fax. Their cover sheet reads: "The family is in . . . Gosh, was it ever out?" Sad to say, but it really was in many circles.

After decades of disruption—characterized by the devaluation of the family, children, and the home by our culture—the family is moving into a new era of respectability. This cultural shift brings new honor back to the role of mother and family manager that should have never been lost. Even Washington has picked up on this new perspective. The Department of Commerce estimated that women's unwaged work in the home is worth over one trillion dollars a year to the U.S. economy. In 1991 members of Congress initiated the Unremunerated Work Act of 1991 to place a dollar value on unpaid housework; they want to include it in the U.S. Gross National Product.

I say this not to imply every woman who works in the marketplace should quit her job and come home. Out of the five best mothers and homemakers I know, one is a physician, one is an interior designer, and the other is a self-employed entrepreneur. These women live balanced lives, and their families take priority over their careers. (I might add that their husbands share that priority.) Their children are a delight to be around. They each have an excellent self-image, and all are self-disciplined and well-behaved.

I know other mothers who do not work outside the home and fritter their time away watching soap operas and shopping—adding stress to their family by running up big credit-card bills. Discontent and bored with their lives, they are not very good mothers because they have low self-esteem and stay in a grumpy frame of mind much of the time.

Every woman who wants to lead a fulfilling life must be true to the gifts and talents God has given her and pursue those abilities as she feels called. She must at the same time balance her personal development with the responsibilities of motherhood. Each of our situations is very different, and every family is unique. But we all have one thing in common. There are days when we scream, "Motherhood and family management is hard work—I need help!" I seem to repeat these words on a regular basis.

When I feel like this, there's a verse in the Bible that gives me comfort. For a woman who sheds enough hair daily to stuff a sofa pillow, Matthew 10:30 is fraught with meaning. This verse says God cares so much about me the very hairs of my head are numbered. This means he has to recount continually!

The way I see it, if God cares about the hair caught in my hairbrush, surely he cares about backed-up plumbing, sick children, overdue bills, leaky roofs, smart-aleck teen-agers, inhumane carpool schedules, and burned dinners. Actually, I believe he cares more than we can imagine because he loves us more than our finite minds can comprehend. The Bible says all I need to do is ask when I feel frustrated or need help (James 1:5). So I only have myself to blame if I don't ask for God's help or heed his advice.

Someone wrote years ago, "Life is meant to provide enough difficulties to show us our need for Christ." Quite frankly, if we started dwelling on all of life's potential calamities, we might run for cover. They're definitely more than we can handle alone. Fortunately, God never intended us to face them alone. He is there with us every step of the way to bring power when we're weak, forgiveness when we fail, hope when we despair, purpose when we're aimless, guidance when we're lost, wisdom when we're confused, acceptance when we're rejected, significance when we feel unimportant, and comfort when we're in pain. As for me, I need all of the above.

But there's one thing he requires of us to receive his help. It's not doing our best (thank goodness!) or all of us would be disqualified. It's not always being honest; who of us is consistently honest? It's not putting others first; much of the time we're selfish. Of course, all of these things please God, but if I for one had to qualify for God's help, I wouldn't get close to meeting the requirements.

His help comes as a gift of grace. It's free. The one requirement is that we give up trying to be superwoman and admit our need of him. Our ultimate need is to reestablish a relationship with our Creator. He is the only one who can help us be the women and mothers we were created to be. The Bible tells us God offers to exchange all our guilt and all our inadequacies for all his forgiveness and all his power through his Son, Jesus Christ. I'm no economist, but I know a deal when I see one. "For God so loved the world that he gave his one and only Son, that whoever believes in him shall not perish but have eternal life" (John 3:16).

The destroyed relationships and hurting families I've witnessed who try to go it alone are incentive enough for me to seek God every day through prayer and reading his instructions for life found in the Bible. I encourage you to do the same. Remember, we're on a divinely commissioned mission.

In the introduction I told you about my three Cs for mothering, which I wrote in my prayer journal some time back: courage, consistency, and commitment. I pray that each and every one of us will find the courage to be consistent in this business of mothering and to renew our commitment to do our best daily.

I've confessed our family's crazy stories and written the ideas in this book in hopes that they will help you build positive relationships with your children and strengthen bonds within your family. I also hope you are encouraged in your powerful role of mother and family manager and in your relationship with God.

I would love to hear about your family. Write to me if you have time between carpools!

Kathy Peel
Creative People, Inc.
P.O. Box 5100
Tyler, Texas 75712

Notes

Chapter 3 ☙ The Self-Disciplined Child, an Endangered Species

1. Zig Ziglar, *Raising Positive Children in a Negative World* (Nashville: Oliver Nelson, 1985), 20.
2. Edith Schaeffer, *What Is a Family?* (Old Tappan, N.J.: Fleming H. Revell, 1975), 80.
3. Tom Landry, *Tom Landry: An Autobiography* (New York: HarperCollins/Zondervan, 1990), 276.

Chapter 6 ☙ Teaching Values to Kids and Other Lost Episodes of "Mission Impossible"

1. Edith Schaeffer, *What Is a Family?* (Old Tappan, N.J.: Fleming H. Revell, 1975), 121, 132.
2. Armand Nicholi, Jr., *What Do We Know about Successful Families?* (n.p., n.d.).

Chapter 7 ☙ Visit to a Dud Ranch: Tips on Making Fun Family Memories

1. Juliet B. Schor, *The Overworked American* (New York: HarperCollins, 1991), 20.

Chapter 8 ☙ Family Finances, or How to Obtain a Loan Using Your Children as Collateral

1. George MacDonald, *The Laird's Inheritance* (reprint, Minneapolis: Bethany House Publishers, 1987).
2. Bruce Baldwin, *Beyond the Cornucopia Kids* (Wilmington, N.C.: Direction Dynamics, 1988).

Chapter 9 ❦ The Stomach Virus and Other Forms of Family Bonding

1. C. S. Lewis, *Mere Christianity* (New York: Macmillan, 1952), 174.